35 OF YOUR FAVORITE WILD ANIMALS
TO FOLD IN AN INSTANT

Wild & Wonderful
ORIGAMI

MARI ONO
& ROSHIN ONO

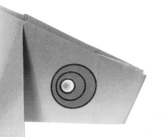

CICO BOOKS
LONDON NEW YORK

Published in 2011 by CICO Books
An imprint of Ryland Peters & Small Ltd

20–21 Jockey's Fields   519 Broadway, 5th Floor
London WC1R 4BW   New York, NY 10012

www.cicobooks.com

10 9 8 7 6 5 4 3 2 1

A CIP catalog record for this book is available from the
Library of Congress and the British Library.

ISBN: 978 1 907563 56 0

Printed in China

Editor: Robin Gurdon
Designer: Paul Tilby
Photographer: Geoff Dann
Stylist: Trina Dalziel

Contents

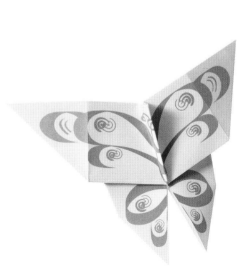

INTRODUCTION

An *origami* model that you've made yourself has a value that no amount of money can replace—every time you create *origami* you're actually giving something of yourself.

If you know how to fold a design, one simple sheet of paper is all you need to give everyone around you a happy feeling. You can have fun changing not just the shape but also the mood of every piece you make and the fun you get from *origami* can be enjoyed anywhere by anybody, without the need for any special tools or equipment. Once you start, there are so many exciting things to make; there is almost nothing that cannot be recreated in *origami*.

In this book we have introduced a series of animals made using both traditional Japanese and modern designs, which will allow you to create your own paper zoo. Also included are specially designed papers, so you can start folding straight away, or you can use plain paper and draw on your own faces and markings.

Please do not be frightened by the instructions in this book: when first seen they might look tricky but you will soon learn that most of the objects are based on the same basic folding patterns that can be repeated time and again. Just remember to make every crease sharp and align every edge perfectly. Once you have practiced, you, too, will soon become an *origami* master!

Now start to experience the *origami* world that everyone can enjoy, regardless of age!

BASIC TECHNIQUES

The most basic skill of *origami* is folding paper precisely and creating strong, straight creases. This can be achieved through concentration and ensuring folded edges and corners match perfectly before firming up creases. To build up models more complicated folds are needed to ensure the paper retains its shape. The four most basic of these are explained here.

INSIDE FOLD

Use this technique to surround one part of the sheet of paper with the rest, enclosing much of the fold between the outer parts of the sheet beneath the fold line.

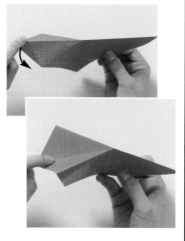

1 Make a fold, here from corner to corner, and then turn down one corner at the intended final angle below the main crease.

2 Lift the sheet and open out the corner that was folded over then push down the outer point of the edge, reversing the crease.

3 When the sheet is flattened the folded corner will be inside the paper with the reverse of the design showing.

OUTSIDE FOLD

Use this technique to enclose the majority of a sheet with one folded corner, pushing the folded tip over the main crease line.

1 Make a fold across the paper, turning the tip over and beyond the fold line.

2 Open out the sheet and fold the corner of the paper up and backward, reversing the creases.

3 When the sheet is flattened the folded corner will be outside the paper with the reverse of the design showing.

SQUARE FOLD

This technique creates a square or diamond shape that can then be used as the basis for any number of *origami* models.

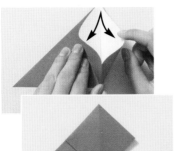

1 Fold the paper from corner to corner then fold the triangle in half again making a right-angled triangle.

2 Lift the top flap and open it out pushing the folded corner away from you, opening the crease and refolding with two new side folds into a diamond shape.

3 Turn the paper over and lift up the other triangular flap, refolding it in the same way so that you are left with a small square or diamond shape.

TRIANGLE FOLD

In contrast to the square fold, the triangle fold starts with a square shape and converts it into a triangle.

1 Fold the paper from side to side then fold it in half again making a square.

2 Lift the top flap and open it out pushing the folded corner away from you, opening the crease and refolding into a triangle with two new side folds and a horizontal top.

3 Turn the paper over and lift up the other triangular flap, refolding it in the same way so that you are left with a triangle shape.

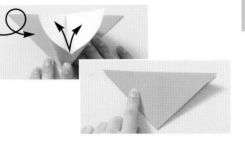

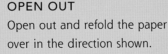

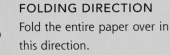

KEY TO ARROWS

OPEN OUT
Open out and refold the paper over in the direction shown.

TURN OVER
Turn the paper over.

FOLD
Fold the part of the paper shown in this direction.

CHANGE THE POSITION
Spin the paper 90° in the direction of the arrows.

MAKE A CREASE
Fold the paper over in the direction of the arrow then open it out again.

FOLDING DIRECTION
Fold the entire paper over in this direction.

CHANGE THE POSITION
Spin the paper through 180°.

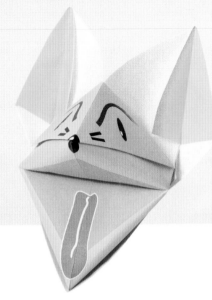

ANIMAL FUN

01 KARASU CROW

The *origami* crow is one of the most commonly made models; it spread across Japan many years ago at the advent of the art. The appearance of a crow in both fairy tales and movies often symbolizes a mysterious or magical feeling and now it's your turn to begin creating your own fantasy world. Making the crow is very simple: use the folds shown in the basic techniques section to produce this standing bird.

Difficulty rating ● ○ ○

You will need
1 sheet of 6in (15cm) square paper

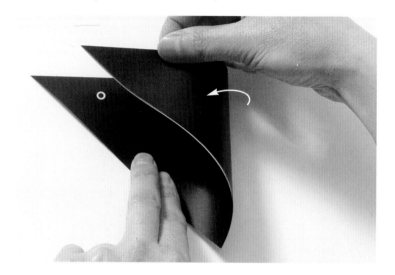

1 Fold the paper in half from corner to corner, making the crease between the eyes, then fold in half again.

2 Lift the top flap and begin to make the square fold (see page 9) by opening out the flap and pressing it down in a diamond shape.

3 Turn the object over and repeat, opening out the top flap and pressing it down to make a diamond.

ANIMAL FUN

12

KARASU CROW

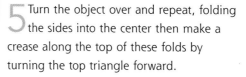

4 Lift the top flaps on each side and fold them in so that their edges align along the central crease.

5 Turn the object over and repeat, folding the sides into the center then make a crease along the top of these folds by turning the top triangle forward.

6 Release the triangle and open out the flaps, then take the tip of the top sheet and fold it back so that the sides meet all along the center line of the object. Turn the paper over and repeat, opening out the flaps, pushing the top point away from you and letting the sides fold in to meet along the center.

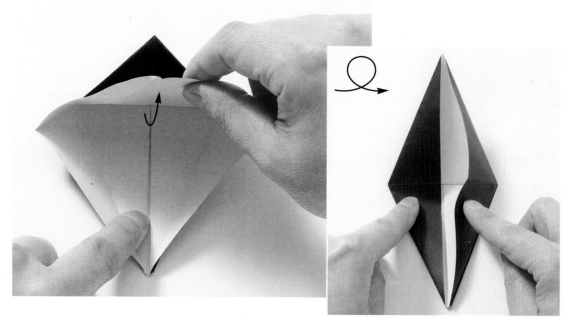

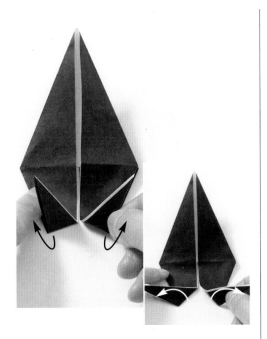

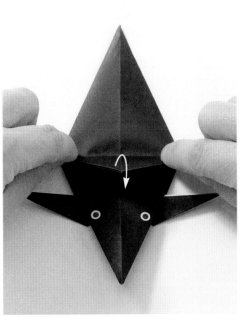

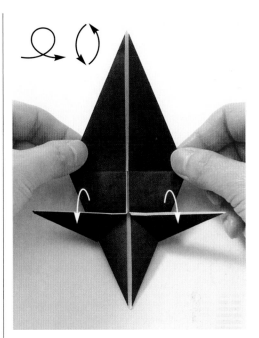

7 Fold up the bottom points at an angle, so that each tip ends up on the side point, and make creases. Now refold so that the points stick out at right angles to the object and make new folds.

8 Fold forward the top half of the object along the middle crease, then also fold forward the small triangle in the middle of the object.

9 Lift the object and turn it over so that the eyes on the paper are under the further point. Now fold forward both inner flaps as shown.

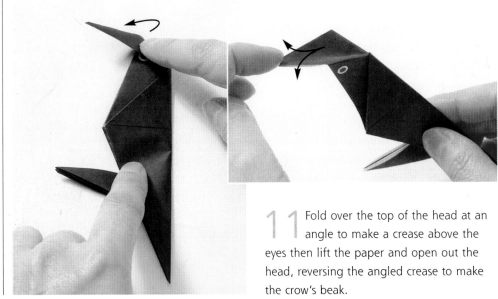

10 Fold the object in half along the main central crease.

11 Fold over the top of the head at an angle to make a crease above the eyes then lift the paper and open out the head, reversing the angled crease to make the crow's beak.

02 TSURU CRANE

The crane is one of the most well-known traditional *origami* designs. A lot of meanings are attributed to the crane: it can symbolize peace, happiness, and good wishes. For instance, if a friend becomes seriously ill, we will make 1,000 *origami* cranes to bring them good luck and ensure their quick recovery. A lot of basic techniques are included in this design— by mastering them you will have all the means you need to become a master of the art of *origami*.

Difficulty rating ● ● ●

You will need
1 sheet of 6in (15cm) square paper

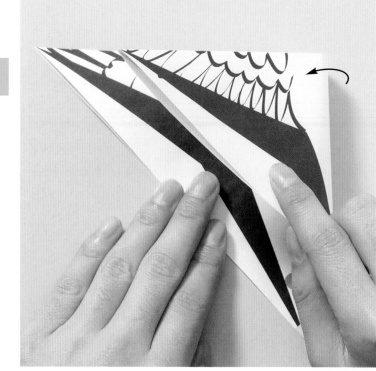

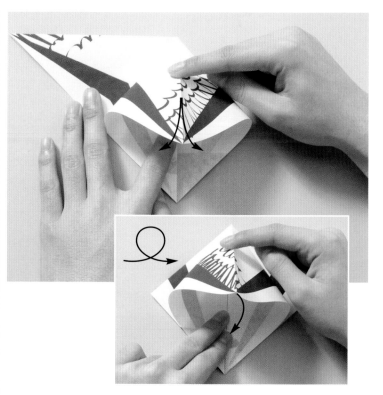

1 With the paper face down and the eyes at the tip, fold the top half of the paper forward from corner to corner, then fold in half again, making the crease between the eyes.

2 Lift the top flap and begin to make the square fold (see page 9) by opening out the flap and pressing it down in a diamond shape. Turn the object over and repeat, opening out the top flap and pressing it down to make a diamond.

3 Lift the top flaps on each side and fold them in so that their edges align along the central crease.

4 Turn the object over and repeat, folding the sides into the center then make a crease along the top of these folds by turning the top triangle forward.

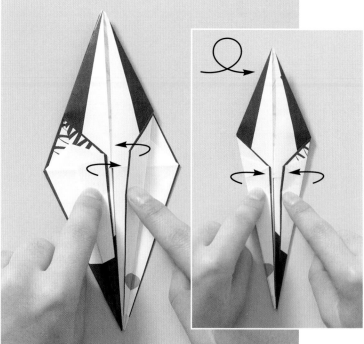

5 Release the triangle and open out the flaps, then take the tip of the top sheet and fold it back so that the sides meet all along the center line of the object. Turn the paper over and repeat, opening out the flaps, pushing the top point away from you and letting the sides fold in to meet along the center.

6 Lift the top flap on each side of the object and fold them into the center so that their edges meet along the center line of the object. Turn the paper over and repeat.

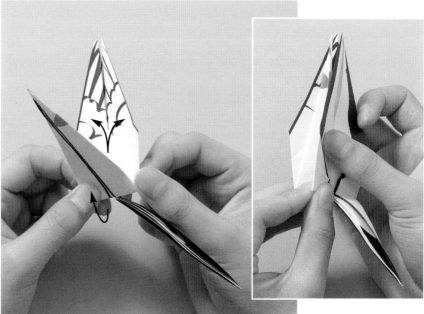

7 Lift the paper and fold up the two lower parts of the object making a crease at the highest possible point. Fold one side back underneath the object, the other forward on top of it.

8 Release the tips then open out the wide part of the object and fold the tips up along the crease made in the previous step, enclosing them inside the wide part of the object. Repeat on the other side.

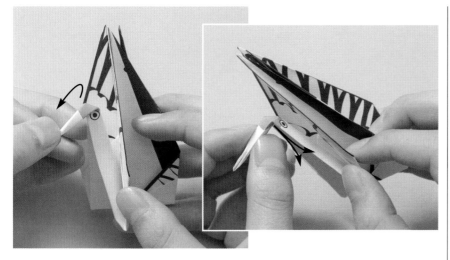

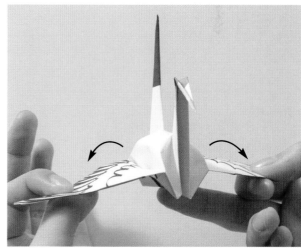

9 Find the point that will make the bird's head and fold over the top at an angle just above the eyes. Now open out the fold and reverse the creases to make the beak.

10 Fold down the wings, making slight creases as close to the body as possible, then gently open out the bird's chest until the wings sit in place.

03 **KITSUNE** FOX

Difficulty rating ● ○ ○

You will need
1 sheet of 6in (15cm) square paper

In Japan the fox is an mystical animal, well-known as one of the country's great gods. The fox itself is a lovely animal that lives most of the time quietly in the beautiful countryside and among the trees of the forest. This mask of the fox's face is easy to make and shows him in a happy mood. You can use it as a puppet, opening and shutting his mouth with your fingers.

ANIMAL FUN

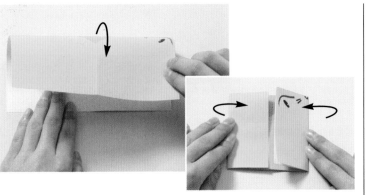

1 Fold the paper in half, open out and refold in the other direction, then fold in both sides so that their edges meet in the middle of the object.

2 Open out the left-hand flap and refold to make a triangle, then repeat on the right-hand flap.

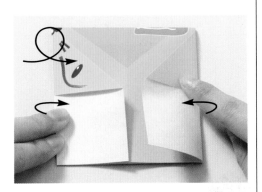

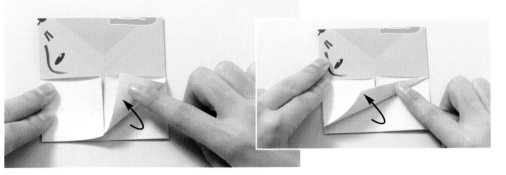

3 Turn the paper over and fold in both sides so that the outer edges meet in the middle of the object.

4 Lift the top flap at the bottom right-hand corner and fold into the center of the object, then make a fold running from the bottom left-hand corner to the middle of the right-hand side ensuring that the top edge of this flap is not horizontal. Turn the object over and repeat on the other side, starting from the left-hand corner.

5 Lift up the object and begin to open it out gently with your thumbs, pressing in the mouth by reversing the horizontal crease as you go.

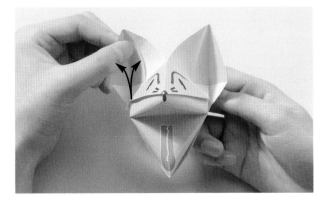

6 Finish by opening out the fox's ears.

04 **KOGUMA** BABY BEAR

This lovely baby bear closely resembles the children's favorite stuffed toy and can be made very easily with just a few creases; it is very simple even allowing for the care needed to successfully balance the face and the body. In addition, a final fold enables it to sit upright on a child's table. Make several baby bear friends from various color *origami* papers and hold a bear tea party or picnic.

You will need
1 sheet of 6in (15cm) square paper

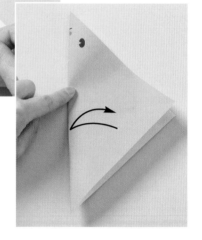

1 Place the paper upside down with the patterned corner furthest away from you then fold the bottom corner away from you. Open out the paper and fold the left corner over to meet the right.

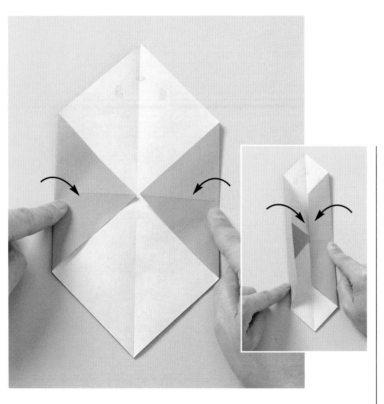

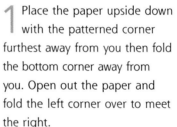

2 Open the paper out. Fold in the two side points so that they meet at the middle and repeat so that the two edges align.

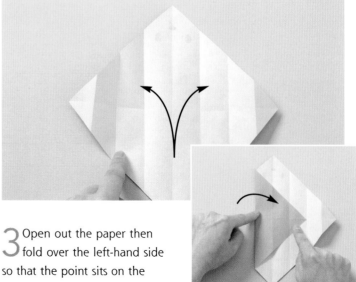

3 Open out the paper then fold over the left-hand side so that the point sits on the second fold from the right.

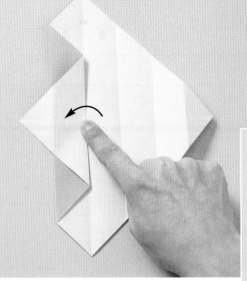

4 Turn the point made in the previous step back to the left so that the fold runs down the paper's central crease, then turn the right-hand point to the left so that it covers the opposite point and turn it back on itself so that the folds run alongside each other.

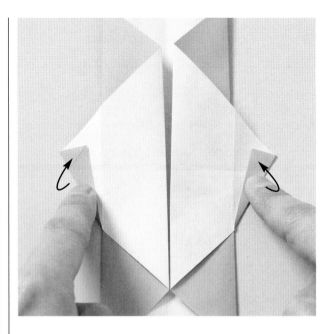

5 Fold over the edges leading up to the outer points, making creases between the place the edges cross the main body of the object and the outer points.

6 Lift up the bottom of the object and open out the lower parts of the two flaps, folding the point up the middle of the paper approximately ½ in (1.25cm) below the top of the flaps and pressing down to make a new crease across the object.

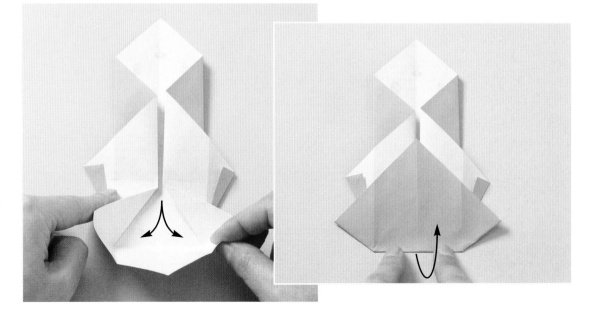

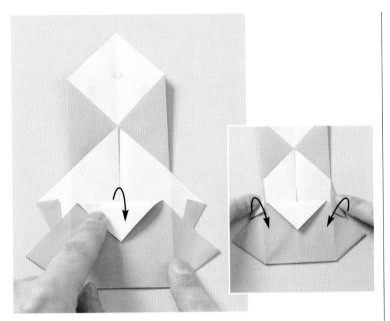

7 Fold down the bottom tip making a crease in line with the object's outer points. Fold these outer tips over at an angle, making new creases between the points where the edges cross the main sides of the object and the side of the bottom flap.

8 Fold forward the top of the paper to make the head, ensuring that the nose just crosses the top of the bottom flap, then tuck the nose underneath making a new horizontal crease.

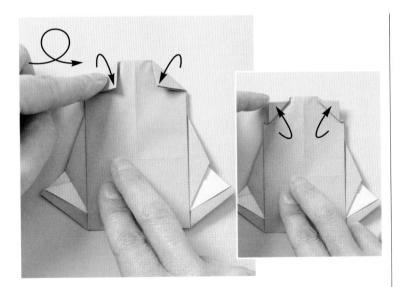

9 Turn the object over and make the ears by folding down the top corners at an angle, then fold them back again about 1/8in (0.25cm) from the new creases.

10 Fold up the bottom ½in (1.25cm) of the object to make a stand for the baby bear.

05 WASHI EAGLE

The sky is ruled by the birds and the most magnificent of them all is the eagle—well-known as the king of the birds. With its huge body and massive wingspan it controls the sky and everything on the ground beneath. Now you can make your own family of these extraordinary birds. Hang them from the ceiling of your room and ensure that these *origami* models control the area as they swing lazily through the air, ready to pounce on unsuspecting prey.

You will need
1 sheet of 6in (15cm) square paper

1 Fold the paper in half to make a crease from corner to corner along the length of the design then open out and make another fold between the side corners. Turn back both tips from the bottom so that they cross the horizontal fold by about ½in (1.25cm), checking that the edges align along the white diagonals in the design.

2 Turn back the top sheet so that the tip crosses the object's bottom edge by about ½in (1.25cm), checking that the design showing through the paper aligns with the bottom of the object. Fold back the other tip on the far side of the object along the edge of the design then turn the flap back about ¼in (0.5cm) from the new tip.

26

ANIMAL FUN

3 Fold the object in half to reinforce the central crease then turn the top flap to the right to make a wing, aligning the new crease along the top of the object's head.

4 Turn the paper over then fold over the other wing to match the first. To finish, open out the object and run your finger along the underside of the wings to give them a curve to resemble flight.

06 **PANDA** PANDA

The panda is an adorable, cuddly animal who eats bamboo every day but unfortunately pandas only live in China so let's see if you can make one and let it live in your own home. To make the model the *origami* paper must first be cut into two pieces. The body is easy to make but the head, with its intricate folds in the small piece of paper, is a little more difficult. When you have folded both join them together with a drop of glue.

You will need
1 sheet of 6in (15cm) square paper
Scissors or scalpel and metal ruler
Paper glue

2 Start making the head with the paper face down. Fold it in half to make a crease then open it out again and fold the sides down and forward at an angle so that the top edges now align along the central crease. Now turn up the bottom edges, making horizontal creases from the angled corners even though these will not necessarily exactly match the edge of the design.

1 Use scissors or a scalpel and metal ruler to divide the sheet into thirds, leaving two thirds for the body and one third for the head of the panda.

3 Turn over the object and pull open the right-hand flap from underneath, then fold it up at an angle so that the bottom edge of the triangle now runs up the center of the object with the rectangular flap to the side. Now repeat on the left-hand side of the object.

28

ANIMAL FUN

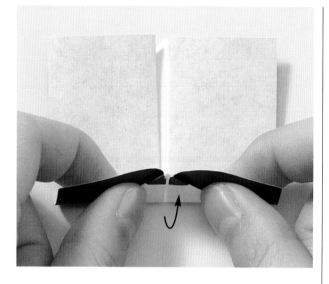

4 Fold up the bottom of the object, making a new crease about ½in (1.25cm) up the paper.

5 With your left forefinger holding down the central triangle lift the right-hand flap and open it out, refolding it so that the corner now sits on the tip of the triangle and a new crease has been made along the bottom of the object. Repeat on the other side.

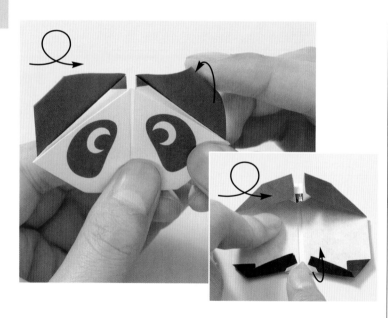

6 Turning the paper over, lift it up and tuck the top corners behind to make the ears, then turn the paper over again and fold back the triangle at the top of the head. This makes the ears angled.

7 Now place the sheet for the body face down and fold in half to make a crease. Turn all four corners in to the center of the object then fold over the tips at either end, ensuring they end up sitting on top of the folded corners.

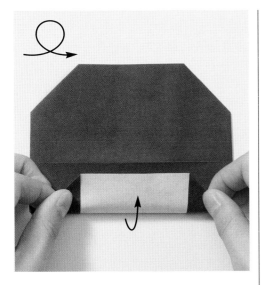

8 Turn the paper over and fold the bottom and top edges over so that they meet along the center crease.

9 Turn the object over again and open out the left-hand flap, refolding it so that the creases reverse and triangles are formed above and below the object. Repeat on the right-hand side.

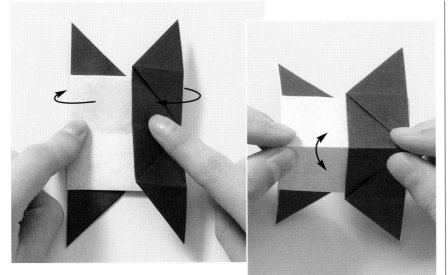

10 Fold over the right-hand side, making a crease along the edge of the folded design, and fold the left-hand side underneath making a similar crease. Now lift the object and fold it in half along the central crease.

11 To finish, slide the head over the right-hand corner of the body and fix in place with a spot of glue.

07 **USAGI** RABBIT

Now it is time for the mischievous rabbit to appear, ready to eat cabbages in the field, and run about the garden. The way this mask is made is a recreation of a traditional *origami* model from Japan. If you put a finger in the upper part of the finished mask and open it out, it is transformed into a candy box with a rabbit's face. To use the mask in this way, press out the bottom part of the rabbit's mask and make a small internal fold to ensure that the box will be steady.

You will need
1 sheet of 6in (15cm) square paper

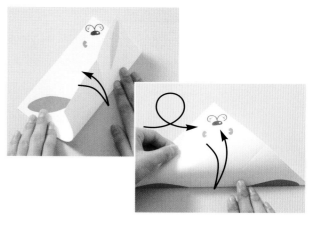

1 Make two creases across the middle of the paper, opening out again each time, then turn over the paper and make a single crease from corner to corner across the design.

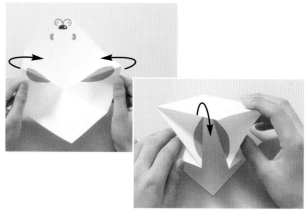

2 Fold in the side points toward each other, at the same time bringing the top point down to the bottom of the object to create a diamond shape.

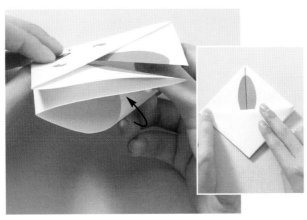

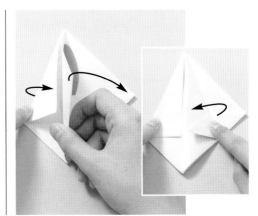

3 Fold the top flap forward, making a crease across the whole width of the paper.

4 Lift up the object and tuck the bottom flap in underneath, again making a crease across the width of the paper. Put the paper back on the table and press the creases in place.

5 Lift the top flap on the left-hand side and turn it over to the right, then fold in the remaining flap on the left so that its top edge runs down the object's central crease. Take the flap you just turned to the right and fold it in so that its edge also runs down the central crease.

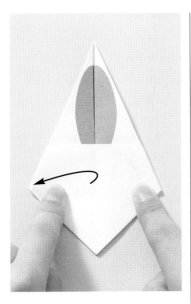

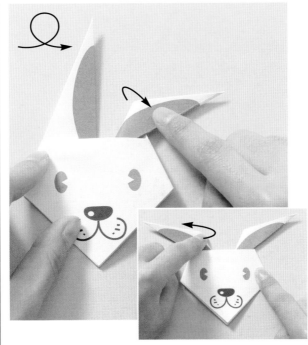

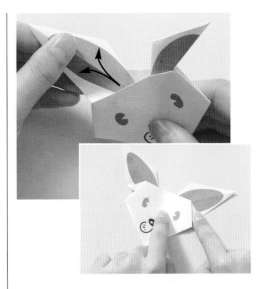

6 Turn the flap you just folded back to the right and then repeat the whole process on the right-hand side of the object, folding in both flaps carefully to meet inside.

7 Turn over the rabbit's ears so that the inner edges touch the corners above the eyes, making folds that run down inside the head.

8 Lift up the object and open out the rabbit's ears by putting a finger inside the ear and twisting the front and back around, then flattening it to make a new crease. Repeat on the other side and press down the small triangles that will have appeared just above the eyes.

SAFARI

08 SHIMA-UMA ZEBRA

Difficulty rating ● ● ●

The herds of zebras that run majestically across the African savannah are one of the greatest sights of a safari. The key to making the zebra is that you should take care to get the right balance between the front and back legs, ensuring the animal stands proudly to attention with its head held high. Now let's reproduce the African plain by making a lot of zebras.

You will need
1 sheet of 6in (15cm) square paper

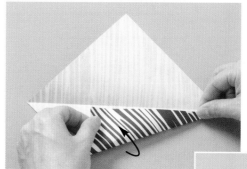

1 Fold the paper from corner to corner across the design and open out. Next fold over the two sides on the left so that their edges meet along the central crease, and repeat on the right.

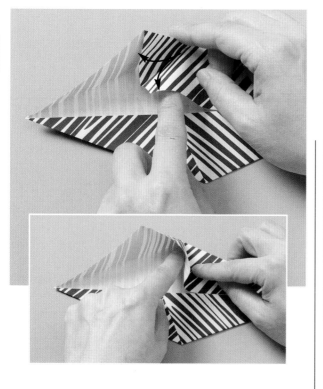

2 Lift the top flap on the left and begin to reverse the inside crease, pushing up the corner of the paper to open out all the folds.

3 Push the corner of the paper to the right so that it sits on the central crease and press down so that the edge of the paper also runs along the central fold. Repeat on the bottom half of the object.

SHIMA-UMA ZEBRA

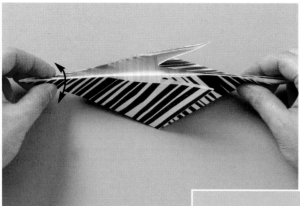

4 Lift up the object and fold it in half lengthwise then place it back on the table with the horizontal edge towards you.

5 Turn the left-hand point so that the bottom edge runs vertically through the object's midpoint and make a crease to form the neck, then open out the object and fold the neck inside, reversing all the creases.

SAFARI

6 Turn over the top of the neck to form the head. Open out the neck and fold the head inside, reversing the direction of the creases.

7 Form the zebra's nose by turning over the tip and making a strong crease then open up the head and fold the tip inside, reversing the folds.

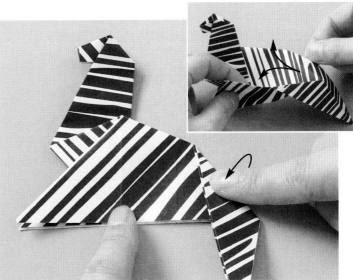

8 Fold the triangular flap beneath the neck forward and repeat on the reverse of the object.

9 Fold down the right-hand end of the object to make the hind legs, ensuring that what was the top edge now runs down at a slight angle. Open out the body of the zebra and reverse the creases, folding the legs around the outside of the body.

10 Fold over the top left-hand triangle to form one of the front legs, again ensuring that the top edge now runs straight down. Repeat on the reverse.

11 Fold back the front edge of the neck, making a vertical crease from the highest point of the head. Lift up the zebra and repeat on the back.

12 To finish, fold up the bottom of the hind legs and make a crease then open out the legs and tuck the tip up inside, reversing the creases.

09 ZOU ELEPHANT

To make an elephant with a happy expression and long trunk, simply cut into the sides of the face with a pair of scissors. Although the folding can at first seem a little tricky, the animal will soon appear in the paper as its face and ears are created with your creases. Once mastered, you can use a smaller sheet of gray paper to make a baby elephant and the family is complete.

Difficulty rating ● ● ●

You will need
1 sheet of 6in (15cm) square paper
Scissors

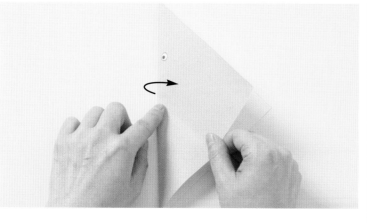

1 With the sheet face down make a crease from corner to corner between the eyes on the design, then open out.

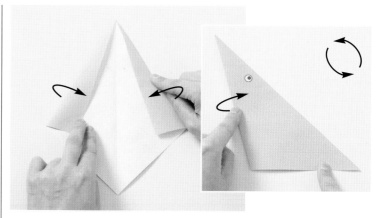

2 Fold in the upper sides, making creases between the top corner and a point approximately 1in (2.5cm) above the side corner, making sure that both sides are identical. Fold the paper in half and twist it so that the shortest side is nearest you.

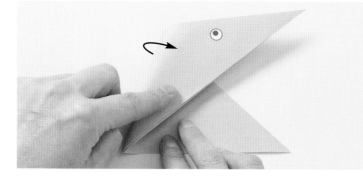

3 Fold the top half of the object to the right, making a crease between the bottom left corner and a point about halfway along the longest edge, ensuring that the new top edge is close to horizontal.

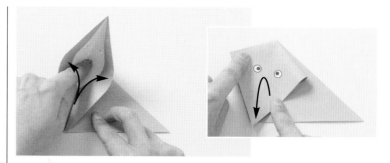

4 Lift the top flap and open it out folding the point forward so that it is in line with the corner of the object underneath.

5 Use the scissors to make small cuts into the top flaps on each side of the face just below the eyes, ensuring they are exactly opposite each other. Fold in the edges of the face from the end of each cut to the bottom point.

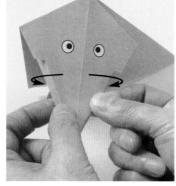

6 Fold the nose back underneath the head between the ends of the cuts, ensuring that the fold is at right angles to the central crease, and then fold the nose back 1/8in (0.25cm) further down. Repeat the double fold 1/2in (1.25cm) nearer the tip of the nose.

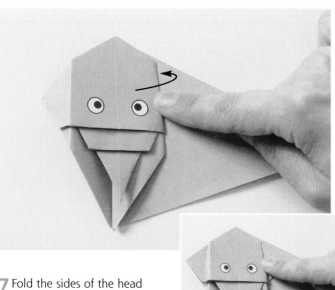

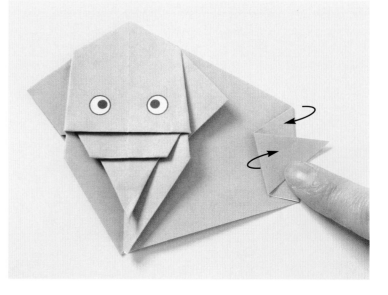

7 Fold the sides of the head underneath making vertical creases, then fold them out again 1/8in (0.25cm) further out to make the ears.

8 Fold back the tail 1 1/2in (4cm) from the corner of the object then fold back the tip so that it ends up well beyond the crease you made first.

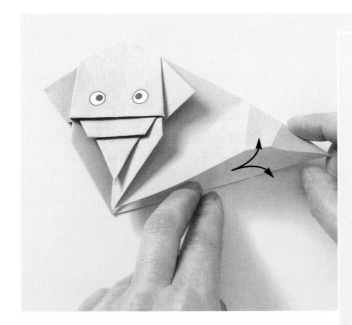

9 Gently open out the back of the object and begin to reverse the large crease so that the tip folds back inside the paper.

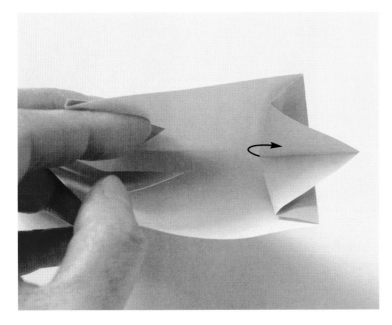

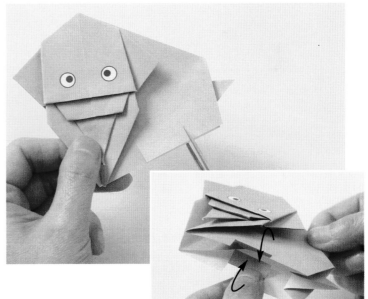

10 Now reverse the second crease so that the tail shows across the crease reversed in the previous step.

11 Use the scissors to cut twice into the bottom of the object then fold up the paper between to make the elephant's legs.

10 **KIRIN** GIRAFFE

The beautiful appearance of a giraffe, who can see from a long distance, is sure to give us the impression that we are truly on a safari. This giraffe is also made from a single sheet of *origami* paper. Start by folding the sheet into the shape of a kite then fold it in on itself using the outside fold (see page 8) to make the giraffe's neck. Next form the body, remembering to ensure the legs are straight and will hold up the model.

Difficulty rating ● ● ○

You will need
1 sheet of 6in (15cm) square paper
Scissors

1 Fold the sheet of paper in half from corner to corner and open out, then fold in the two upper edges so that they meet along the central crease. Fold the paper in half along the crease.

2 Fold the top point down and across to the left, making a diagonal crease up and across the paper from just above the right-hand point.

SAFARI

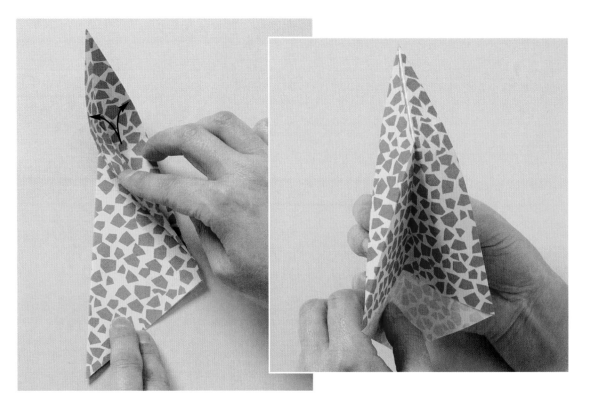

3 Open out the paper and reverse the creases made in the previous step, refolding the paper so that the flap now surrounds the main body of the object.

4 Fold over the tip of the flap and make a crease, then open the flap out, reverse the creases just made, and refold so that the tip surrounds the rest of the flap.

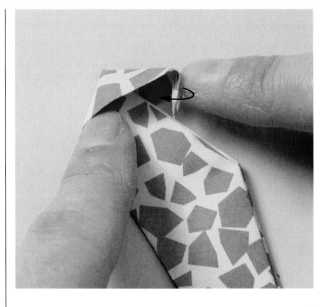

5 Fold the tip over again about ¼ in (0.5cm) from the end and reverse the creases, so that the tip can be folded inside.

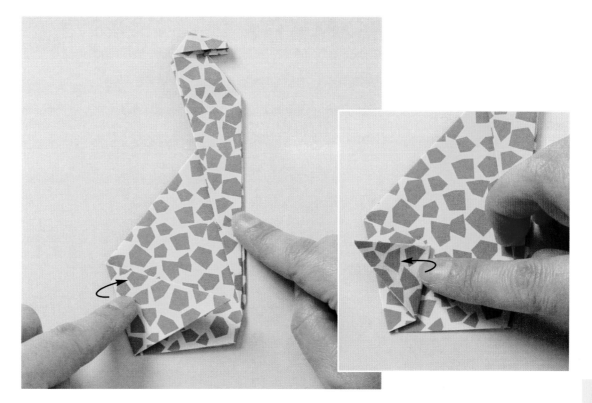

6 Turn over the bottom left corner at a slight angle by about 1in (2.5cm) and make a crease to begin making the giraffe's tail. Turn over the tip a second time so that the corner points up slightly and sticks out from the object.

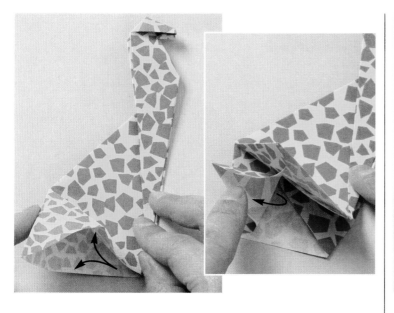

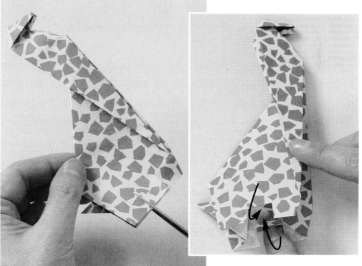

7 Open out the bottom of the object and fold in the tail, reversing the first crease made in the previous step, then reverse the second crease so that the tail sticks out from inside the object.

8 Cut twice through the bottom edges of the object and fold up the loose paper to reveal the giraffe's legs.

11 **SARU** MONKEY

Pleasant, happy monkeys are particularly well-known for the amusing looks they give their companions as their large families scramble through the trees. To make one of these friendly *origami* monkeys all you need are the most basic techniques, but as you finish the model give the monkey expression by choosing one of the various positions for its arm—either bent so that he can hang from a branch, in a folded position, or ready to eat a banana.

You will need
1 sheet of 6in (15cm) square paper
Scissors

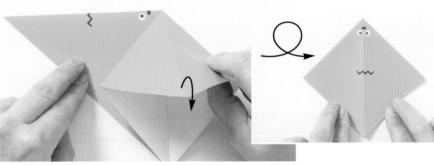

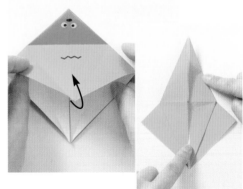

1 Fold the paper in half from corner to corner through the middle of the design, then fold it in half again.

2 Make a square fold (see page 9) by lifting the top flap, opening it out and refolding so the point sits on top of the bottom of the paper. Turn the paper over and repeat so that the object is shaped like a diamond.

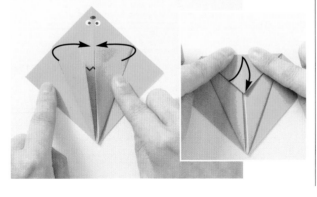

3 Fold the upper flap on each side of the object in so that the edges meet along the central crease, then turn over the top triangle along the top of these folds and release to make a crease.

4 Open out the flaps made in the last step and lift the top sheet, pushing the point away from you. Refold so that a long diamond is formed.

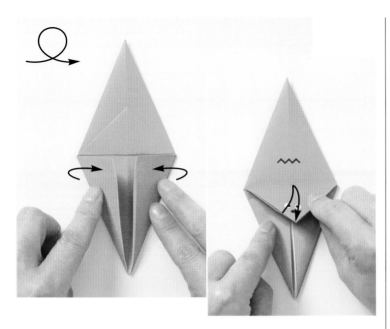

5 Turn the paper over and fold in the bottom two edges as before so that they meet along the central crease, then fold forward the triangle in the middle of the object to make a crease and release.

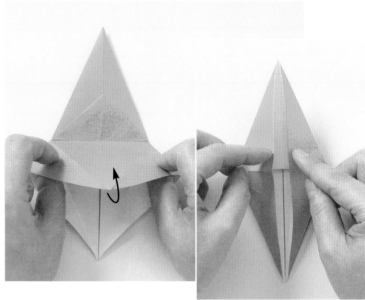

6 Repeat step 5, opening out the flaps and pushing the corner of the paper to the top of the object, flattening the sides to make a thin diamond shape.

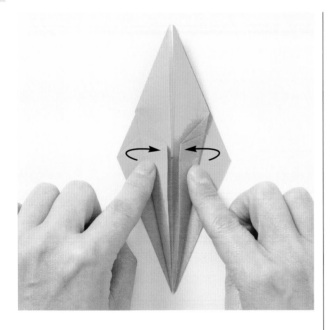

7 Fold in the top flaps on each side so that the lower edges meet along the object's central crease.

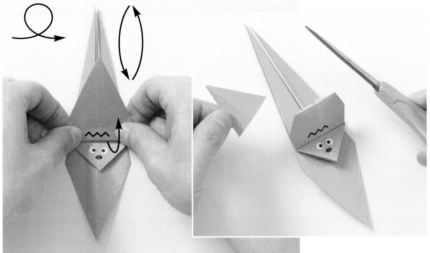

8 Turn the object over and repeat the previous step, folding the edges into the center to match, then spin the paper through 180° and lift the flap nearest you to the vertical and make a crease. Next cut off the top of the flap with the scissors about 1in (2.5cm) from the crease.

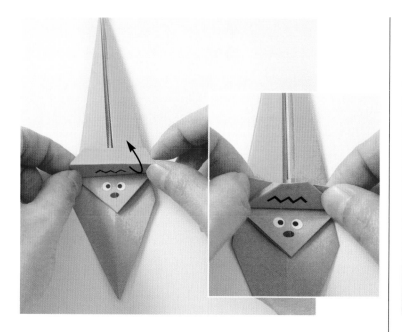

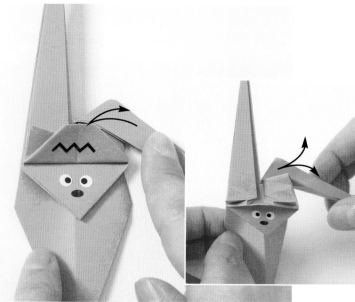

9 Fold over the top of the head, making a crease about 3/8in (1cm) from the end, then fold back the corners before making a second crease and folding them out again to make the ears.

10 Turn over the right-hand arm and make a crease then open out the arm and reverse the creases, folding the end inside.

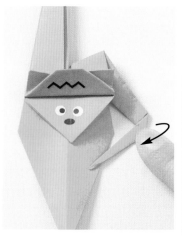

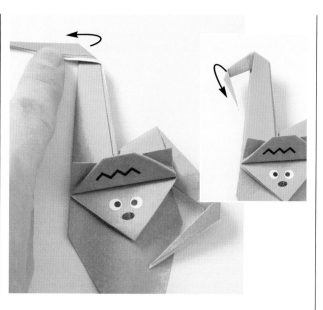

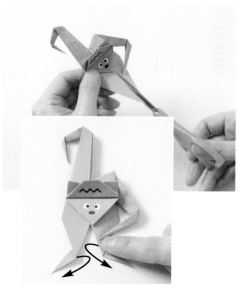

11 Repeat further down the arm to make the elbow, making the crease about halfway along the arm so that the end crosses over the body when folded.

12 Repeat the two creases and reverse folds on the other arm, making both creases much closer to end to indicate a hanging arm.

13 Use the scissors to cut up the body then fold the ends underneath at a slight angle to make the legs.

12 **LION** LION

The lion is the king of beasts and the animal that is most closely associated with the African plains. Seeing these magnificent animals stalk through the undergrowth before bringing down their prey is a scene that can only be witnessed on safari. This *origami* model shows the lion with its mane and a face of concentration. Now let's see if you can create a perfect *origami* lion and yourself become the king of the jungle!

Difficulty rating ● ● ●

You will need
1 sheet of 6in (15cm) square paper

1 Fold the paper in half through the middle of the design, then open it out and fold in the right-hand edges so that they both meet along the central crease.

2 Fold each flap's short edge underneath itself, making a crease from the top and bottom corners to a point about 1in (2.5cm) down the long edge.

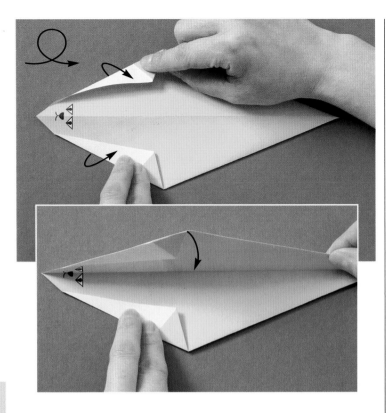

SAFARI

54

3 Next turn over the paper and fold each short edge over, making a crease from beside the nose to a point 1in (2.5cm) beyond the top and bottom corners, then fold the paper in half.

4 Fold over the left-hand tip, making a diagonal crease from a point two-thirds of the way along the lower edge so that the tip folds down and towards the right.

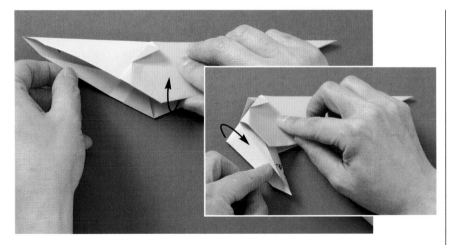

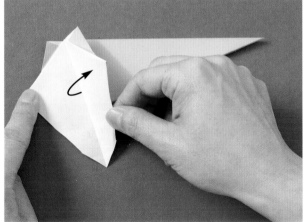

5 Lift the top flap from the bottom and bring the left-hand point across and down, folding it inside the object so that the creases are reversed.

6 Lift the top flap on the object's left-hand side and fold it to the right to make a diamond shape.

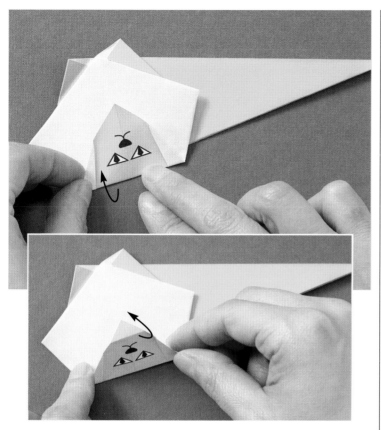

7 Turn over the bend of this diamond to form the lion's face, making a crease about ¼ in (0.5cm) out from the object's main edge and in line with it. Then turn over the tip of the face to form a flat chin.

8 Fold over the tail so that the crease is angled slightly upward, then make three more folds along its length to form the curls of the tail.

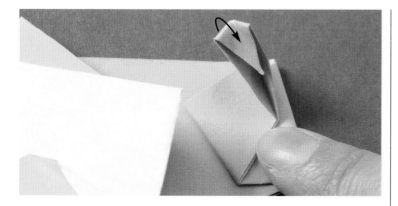

9 Open out the last fold in the tail and turn the end inside, reversing the creases so that it sits flat.

10 Turn the flap below the head across the main edge of the object and make a crease. This edge should sit away from the back of the object and act as a stand for the model.

13 KAMEREONN CHAMELEON

The chameleon is one of the most weird and wonderful creatures on earth, able to change the color of its skin to suit its environment. Watch it move from green to yellow to blue at will, always hiding from its enemies. These chameleons are quiet today on the tree branch waiting to catch insects for food—they are like the *ninja* in Japan. Making this *origami* model is quite easy, though it is crucial to position the face correctly.

Difficulty rating ● ● ○

You will need
1 sheet of 6in (15cm) square paper

1 With the design face down and the eyes on the left, fold the paper in half from left to right, make a crease and open it out again. Repeat the fold from top to bottom, again opening the sheet out afterwards.

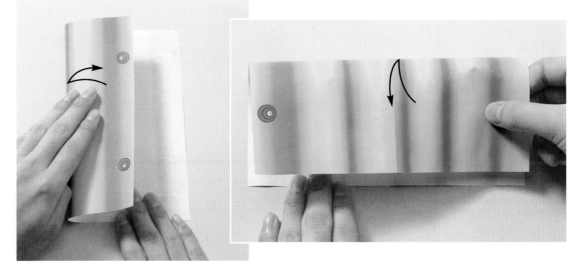

2 Fold the top and bottom edges so that they meet along the horizontal crease then fold in both ends so that they also meet in the middle, make creases, then open them out.

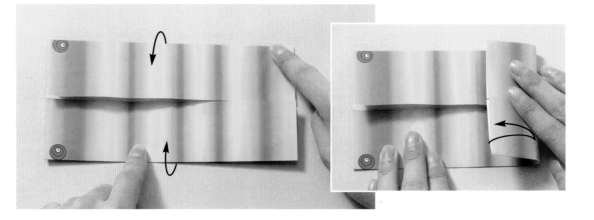

SAFARI

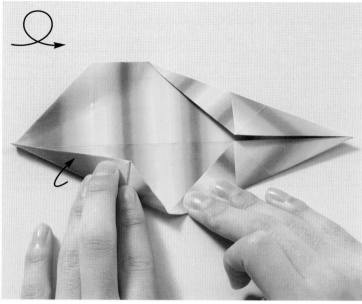

3 Make a pair of triangle folds at each end (see page 9) by lifting one side of the top flap of paper at a time, folding the corner across the crease made in the previous step to the middle of the object, and refolding it to form a triangle.

4 Turn the paper over and fold in the four diagonal edges, starting at the right-hand side, so that the two at each end meet along the central crease.

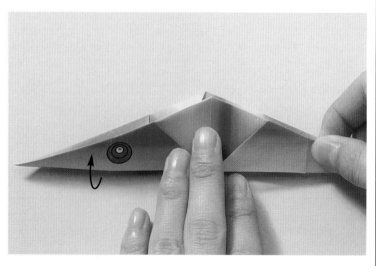

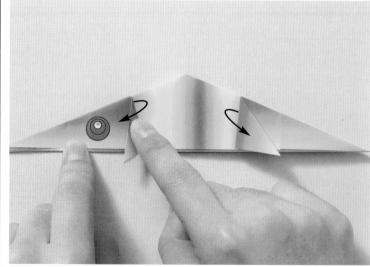

5 Fold the bottom of the object over, reversing the central crease.

6 Fold over the two loose triangles on each side of the object to form the chameleon's legs. Ensure that one side of the triangle is vertical even though this means the tips of the triangles will fall below the main edge of the object.

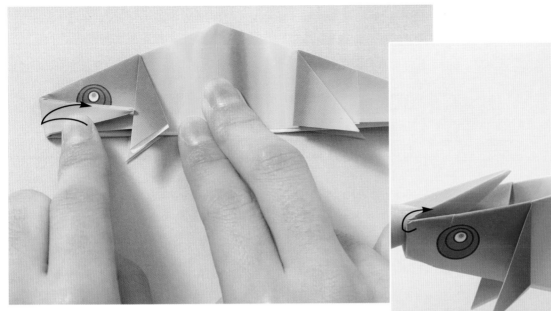

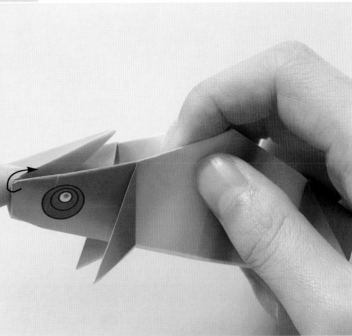

7 Fold back the nose so that the tip touches the model's front leg and make a vertical crease, then open out the body and fold the tip back inside, reversing the creases.

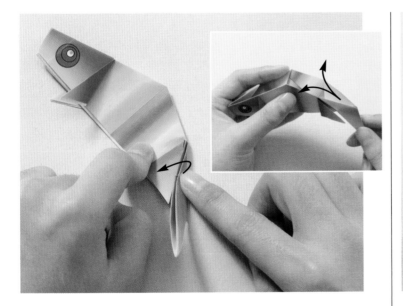

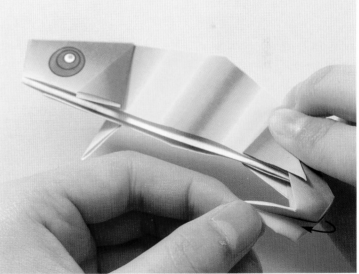

8 Fold forward the tail of the object at an angle, then open out the body and reverse the creases so that the tail surrounds the body of the model.

9 Make another fold in the tail and open it out to reverse the creases so that the tip is surrounded by the bulk of the tail.

14 WANI CROCODILE

Difficulty rating ● ● ○

You will need
1 sheet of 6in (15cm) square paper

The crocodile is often described as a dinosaur that has survived to the present day. Its aggressive stare ensures other wild animals don't come too near while its powerful teeth and jaws will knock down any prey with a single snap. The crocodile is sometimes seen as the rival of the lion so see if you can make one and test how strong it really is!

1 Follow the instructions for the Chameleon (see page 56) folding the paper in half both ways then folding in the top and bottom edges to meet along the horizontal crease, and both ends so that they also meet in the middlet.

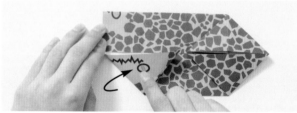

2 Open out the creases made at the end of the previous step and make a pair of triangle folds at each end (see page 9) by lifting one side of the top flap of paper at a time, folding the corner across the crease made in the previous step to the middle of the object, and refolding it to form a triangle.

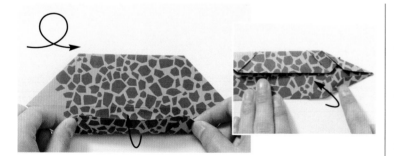

3 Turn the paper over and fold over the top and bottom edges so that they meet along the center crease, then turn over the short diagonal edges on the right of the object so that they also meet along the main crease.

4 Fold the model in half along its length and fold out the two small triangles on each side to form the crocodile's legs. Finally give the tail a curve by curling it around your finger.

15 HEBI SNAKE

Let's make a charming *origami* snake. It may surprise you that there are over 3,000 different kinds of snakes and this book will show you how to make one of them—but only if you are brave enough! The design is made with a special zigzag form—known as *kunekune* in Japanese—that resembles the reptile slithering across the ground.

Difficulty rating ● ● ○

You will need
1 sheet of 6in (15cm) square paper

1 Fold the paper in half from corner to corner to make a crease between the eyes. Open out again and fold in the two right-hand edges so that they meet on the central crease, then repeat so that the two creased edges meet.

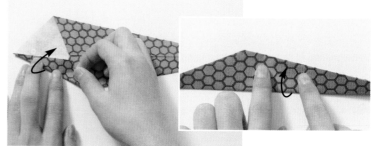

2 Now fold in the two short edges on the right-hand end of the paper so that they also meet in the center, then fold the object in half.

3 Keeping the head still, fold the body underneath at an angle, starting about 3in (7.5cm) from the left-hand tip. Next, fold the body over again three more times in the same direction, ensuring that the sections are all a similar length. Now open up the object and reverse each set of creases in turn starting at the head. When each one is complete hold it in place as you move along the model.

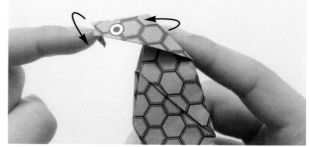

4 To finish make a pair of creases across the head about 1½in (3.5cm) from the tip of the nose, reverse them, and then fold up the tip inside to give the model a flat nose.

SAFARI

16 GORIRA GORILLA

Difficulty rating ● ● ●

You will need
1 sheet of 6in (15cm) square paper

The gorilla is one of the rarest species on earth as well as one of the most popular in the zoo. But what do they do during their days in the wild? When not eating the grass, fruits, and insects they are walking on their knuckles. This *origami* model—showing the gorilla in this pose—is a traditional design from Japan. Although it is challenging to make the first time, it is unexpectedly easy to remember and make again.

1 Fold the paper in half from corner to corner, then open it out and repeat in the other direction. Open out again and fold in half both ways across the sheet, then fold all four corners in so that they meet at the center point.

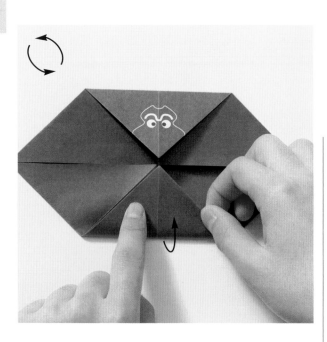

2 Turn the paper through 45° and fold in the top and bottom corners, ensuring that one of them includes the design for the gorilla's face.

3 Turn the paper over and fold the bottom right-hand corner up to the center point, ensuring that the bottom right edge now runs vertically along the object's central crease line. Repeat on the left-hand side.

GORIRA GORILLA

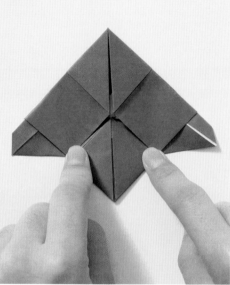

4 Make angled creases on the upper flaps from the model's outer points to the center and fold the flaps over.

5 Now fold the top left- and right-hand corners down to the center point so that the object resembles an arrow head.

6 Lift the upper right-hand flap and reverse the inner crease, before flattening the flap and folding the reversed sheet around the outside. Repeat on the left-hand side.

7 Turn the object over and carefully fold it in half along the central vertical crease.

8 Make the model's feet by opening up the flap in the middle of the object and folding the long edge over. The feet and legs will not fold flat—let them splay open.

9 Gently open out the body then make a crease across the face and reverse the folds to make the gorilla's nose.

10 Fold up the bottom ½ in (1.25cm) of the object to make a stand for the gorilla.

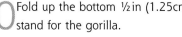

17 **CHIITA** CHEETAH

The cheetah is strong and wild and, as the fastest animal on earth, is so fast that no animal on the African plain is able to keep up with it. The cheetah is a big cat but will your *origami* model be like a pussy cat or a terrifying hunter? Take care when making the model's head as the different creases and folds can become a little confusing. However, all will come out correctly if you follow the instructions slowly and carefully.

Difficulty rating ● ● ●

You will need
1 sheet of 6in (15cm) square paper
Scissors

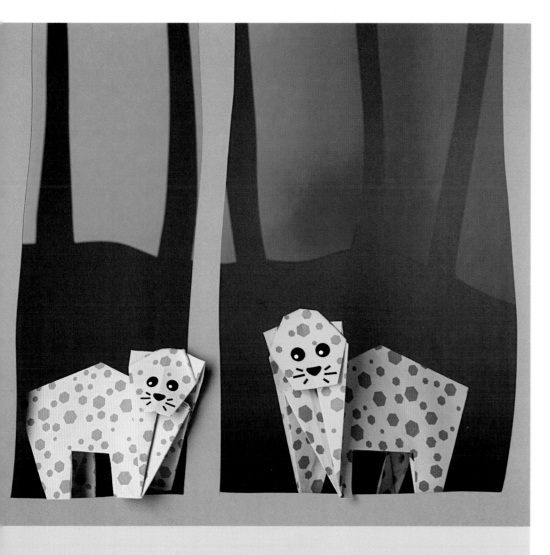

1 Fold the paper in half from corner to corner through the design of the face, then fold in the edges at the face so that they meet along the central crease.

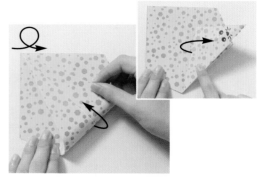

2 Turn the paper over and fold up the narrow point to the opposite corner and make a crease, then fold the narrow point down to the right so that the left-hand edge now runs along the bottom of the object.

3 Pick up the paper and fold the left-hand side of the object underneath along the central crease, then fold the narrow point to the left so that its top long edge turns over and sits on top of the other edge. Fold what is now the upper edge of the long point over from the object's bottom right-hand corner and make a crease so that the tip stands up vertically.

4 Bend the head forward so that it aligns with the crease down the model's neck and turn the nose underneath to form a flat chin. Next turn back the top corners before turning them back on themselves again to form the ears.

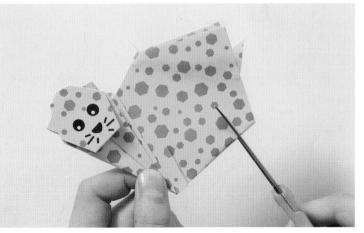

5 Fold over the right-hand corner at an angle then turn it back on itself so that the tip crosses the new crease. Open up the back of the model and fold the tail inside, reversing the crease.

6 Use scissors to make two cuts into the bottom of the model and fold up the flap created to leave the cheetah's front and back legs.

SEA WORLD

18 AZARASHI SEAL

Difficulty rating ● ● ○

You will need
1 sheet of 6in (15cm) square paper

Always a popular animal in the aquarium and the zoo, the seals perform some of the most difficult tricks and are funny and amazing at the same time, proving they are intelligent—perhaps even intelligent enough to make a *origami* seal as well? When you have folded the body of the model it might seem that the animal is finished, but you must remember to bend the head and the tail—only then does it become an intelligent seal.

SEA WORLD

1 Fold the sheet in half from corner to corner, then open up and fold the two right-hand edges in so that they meet each other along the central crease. Now turn the paper over and fold the narrow point over to the wide point.

2 Turn the paper back over and fold out both flaps by lifting each vertical edge and folding the points to the right, making a new edge all along the central crease. Now lift the top point on the left and fold it to the right to make a diamond shape.

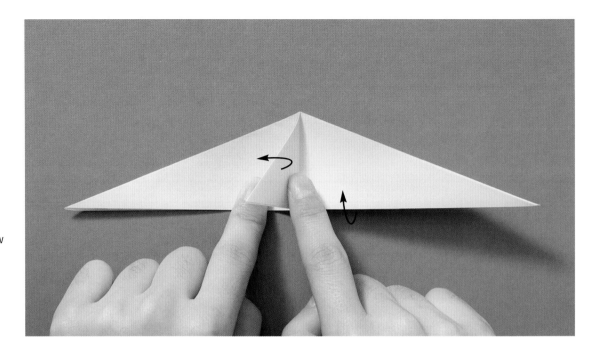

3 Fold the bottom half of the object up along the central crease and fold the triangle now in the middle to the left. Turn the object over and repeat so that both triangles now point towards the head, then turn the object back over.

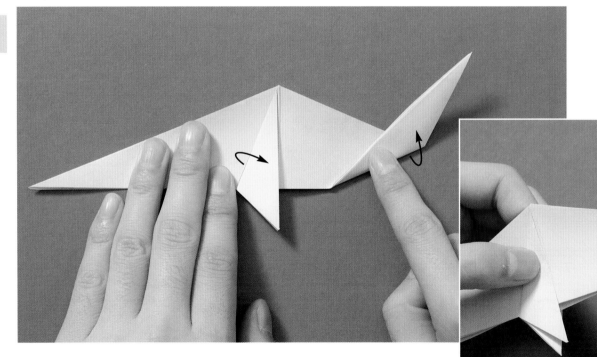

4 Fold the central triangle on both sides in half, back to the center of the object. Next fold the right-hand end up at an angle and make a crease, then open out the model and turn the flap inside, reversing the creases to make the tail.

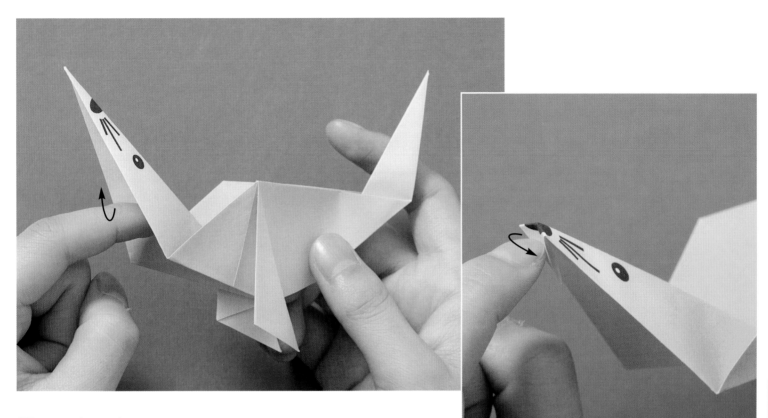

5 Repeat the previous step at the other end to form the head, making the first fold at a lesser angle but nearer the center of the object. Next fold it inside the object, reversing the folds.

6 To finish, turn up the ends of the central triangles to make flat feet.

19 FUGU BLOWFISH

The gently swelling blowfish—one of Japan's greatest delicacies—is famous for its taste but remember to be careful, as the wrong parts are very poisonous if eaten! You might notice that this model closely resembles the traditional *origami* balloon—both need to be blown up to make their shape—but you can also use your finger to give it the ideal shape.

Difficulty rating ● ● ●

You will need
1 sheet of 6in (15cm) square paper

SEA WORLD

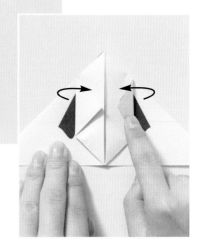

1 Fold the paper in half between the eyes and in half again making a crease, then lift the top flap and make a triangle fold (see page 9) on both sides.

2 Fold up the outer points of the upper flaps so that they meet at the top point, forming a diamond, then fold in the outer points of the diamond to meet on the center line.

3 Fold down the two loose tips at the top of the object so that their edges run along the edges made in the previous step. Tuck these doubled-over flaps into the pockets on the diagonal edges and flatten.

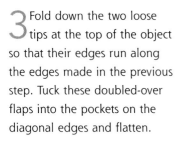

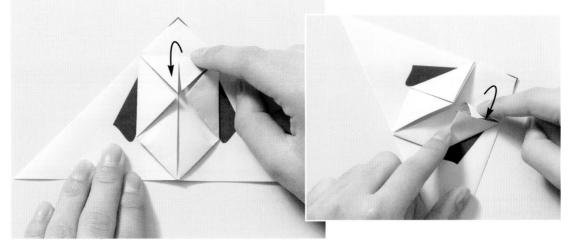

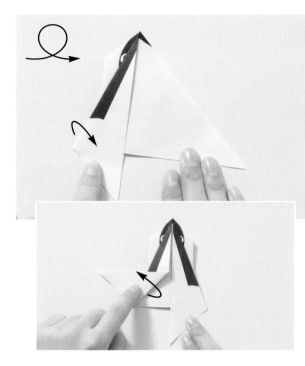

4 Turn the model over and fold each side in half so that their diagonal edges align along the center line, then fold the bottom left-hand tip back out to the sides making a crease from the outer corner to the center line.

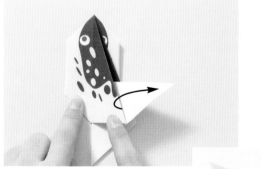

5 Fold over the left-hand tip, along with the flap running up to the top of the object, then pick it up and loosen the body with your fingers before blowing gently into the model to inflate it.

20 RAKO SEA OTTER

Difficulty rating ● ○ ○

A lovely sea otter is always everyone's favorite. They slip gracefully into the water and glide through the sea while looking for food among the rocks and seaweed. When they find their food they can easily open any shell, before eating like a nibbling rabbit. This sea otter's *origami* model is very easy to make, so with a single sheet of *origami* paper you can make your own version of this adorable creature.

You will need
1 sheet of 6in (15cm) square paper

1 Fold the paper in half from corner to corner to make a crease then open out and repeat in the other direction. Fold the bottom corner up to the center point and make a crease, then open up and refold so that the crease now runs along the center line.

2 Open out the paper again and fold down the top point so that it sits on the middle crease of the three creases, then fold back the bottom along this same crease.

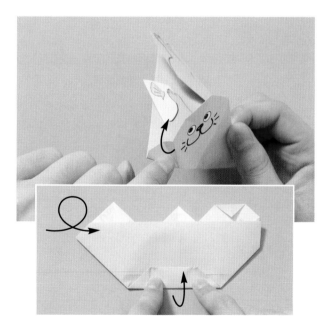

3 Turn up the right-hand end so that the bottom is vertical and the bottom right-hand point now sits on the diagonal line where it changes color. Turn up the left-hand end in the same way but ensure that the left-hand corner now sits on the point where the diagonal edge crosses the horizontal.

4 Turn over the top of the head to make a flat crease then fold over the left-hand tip to make a short vertical crease, before opening out the body and folding it inside, reversing the creases. Turn the model over and fold up the bottom to make a stand.

21 **KUJIRA** WHALE

This big whale is easy to make yet it clearly shows the animal's gentle character as well as its strength and intelligence. An actual whale is the biggest animal in the world and spends its life cruising gently through the oceans as it travels vast distances across the world. Each individual whale is very valuable as a crucial part of the cycle of nature. Now let's see if you can make the whale as it was seen in the film of the story of Pinocchio!

Difficulty rating ● ○ ○

You will need
1 sheet of 6in (15cm) square paper

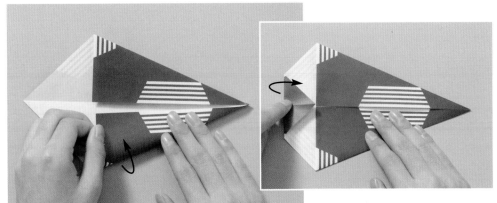

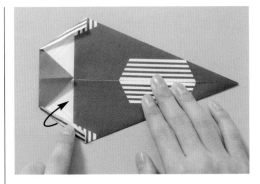

2 Fold over the short diagonal edges from the ends of the left-hand triangle, following the design.

1 Fold the paper in half between the eyes and open out, then fold in the top and bottom points so that the edges meet along the central crease. Fold back the left-hand point to the folded edge.

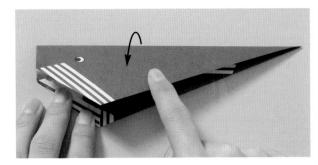

3 Fold forward the top of the model along the central crease.

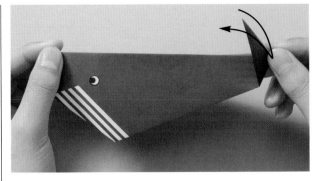

4 Turn over the end of the tail at a sharp angle and make a crease, then open out the body, fold the tail inside and reverse the creases.

22 **UMIGAME** SEA TURTLE

The sea turtle swims gracefully through the sea with a gentle flap of its fins. It is an animal familiar to all Japanese children since it appears in a famous old fairy tale. When you make the model don't forget to tuck in the corners of the shell so that it more closely resembles the real thing. When cutting the paper to create the front legs, take care to cut right to the center of the paper, but without slicing into any part of the shell.

Difficulty rating ● ● ○

You will need
1 sheet of 6in (15cm) square paper
Scissors

1 With the design face down and with the pattern on the right, fold the top point down to the bottom then the right-hand point to the left.

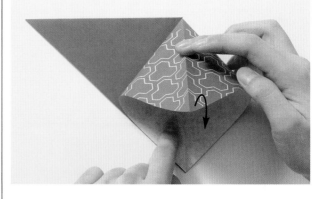

2 Lift the top flap, open it out and refold it to make a square fold (see page 9).

3 Turn the paper over and repeat the square fold to form a diamond, then fold in the two upper flaps from the side points so that the edges meet along the centre line from the bottom up.

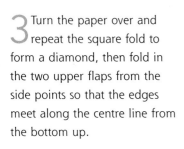

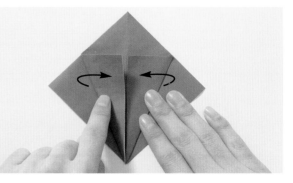

4 Fold the top triangle forward over the edges made in the previous step to make a crease and release, then open out the flaps and fold back the bottom point to make a narrow diamond.

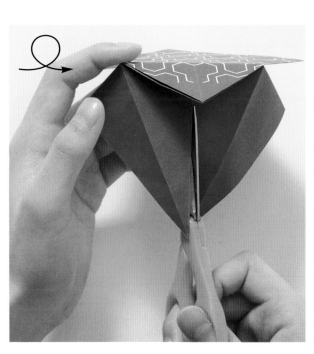

5 Lift up and turn over the object letting the diamond shape reopen slightly. Use scissors to cut down the center of the loose flap to the point where it meets the main bulk of the object, then reform the narrow diamond.

6 Fold back the separated points of the diamond at an angle so that they end up close to the model's outer points. Next fold back the head, as close to the two arms as possible, then turn it back on itself leaving a concertina fold.

7 Turn the tips of the arms back on themselves then open them out and fold the tips inside, reversing the creases.

8 Fold both side points toward the center ensuring that the tips touch the diagonal creases running down to the bottom of the model.

9 Fold out the upper flaps from the bottom point, then turn back the remaining point at the bottom to make a concertina fold to form the tail.

23 **PENGUIN** PENGUIN

It's possible to reproduce almost every animal in the world with *origami*, even the penguins that live among the ice in the Antarctic Ocean. It is unexpectedly easy to make this model so that the bird stands erect as it does when venturing onto land. Turning the position of the face will allow each bird to balance in a different way, as well as giving each one his own character. Make a number of birds to stand together and try using a smaller sheet of paper to make a baby, which will complete the family.

Difficulty rating ● ● ●

You will need
1 sheet of 6in (15cm) square paper

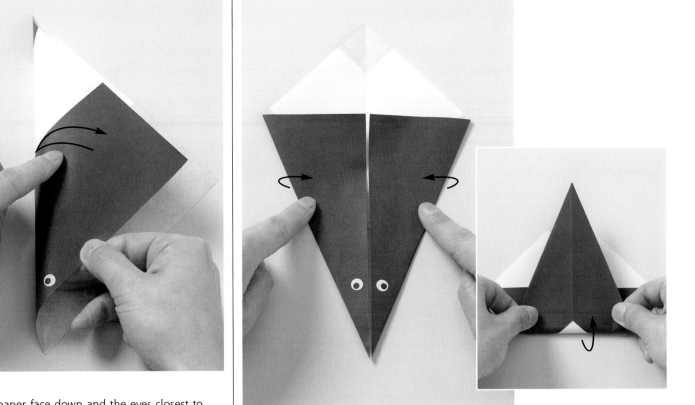

1 With the paper face down and the eyes closest to you, fold the sheet in half to make a crease from corner to corner through the middle of the design, then open it out again.

2 Fold the two side points in so that the edges meet along the central crease, then fold the bottom tip up so that it sits on top of the top tip.

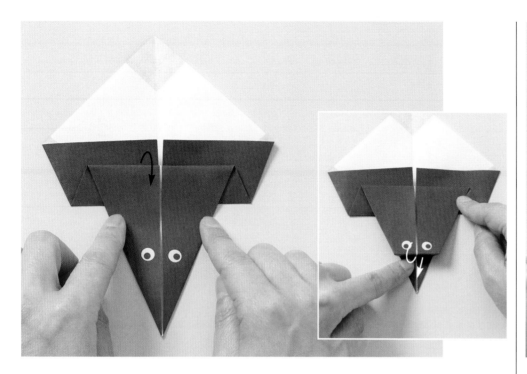

3 Fold back the upper tip, making a second crease halfway across the colored part of the paper showing, then turn the nose underneath just below the eyes. Turn it back again, making another crease ½in (1.25cm) closer to the tip.

4 Fold the object in half right along the central crease.

5 Turn back the bottom left tip of the main part of the model, making a crease from the left-hand tip to a point ½in (1cm) from the right-hand edge. Turn the object over and repeat before turning it back again.

6 Turn the bottom of the object over to the right, using the diagonal edge as a guide for the crease line.

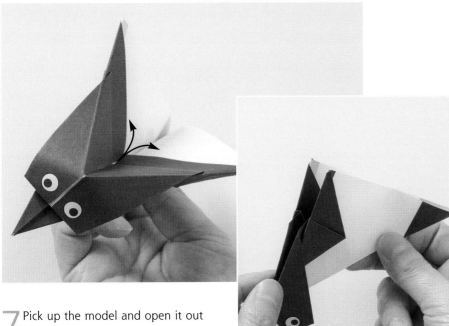

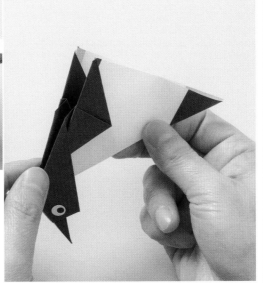

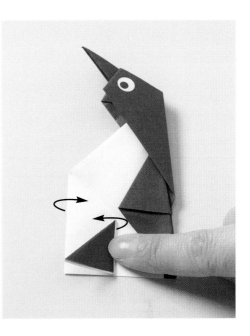

7 Pick up the model and open it out slightly, turning the head downward. Close up the model again, reversing the creases, and make an outside fold to form the penguin's head.

8 Fold over the bottom left-hand corner to make a vertical crease, then turn the tip back again so that it just crosses the fold just made.

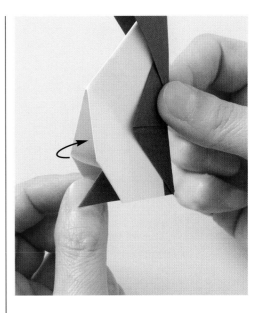

9 Open out the body and fold the tip inside, reversing the larger creases, but leave the tip protruding. Close the object back up.

10 Fold the bottom corners inside at an angle to show more of the feet.

24 IRUKA DOLPHIN

The dolphin is one of the most beautiful mammals in the world, living in families called pods that roam the vast expanse of the ocean. The body of the dolphin is almost like a rainbow weaving its way through the sea, creating a fabulous sight as it leaps through the surf showing off its glistening body. When beginning to fold this *origami* model, first make the important pair of intersecting creases upon which the entire shape of the dolphin is based.

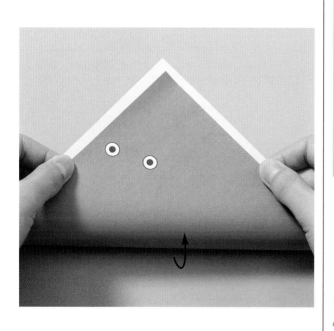

Difficulty rating ● ● ●

You will need
1 sheet of 6in (15cm) square paper

1 With the design face down fold the paper in half from corner to corner.

2 Turn over the left-hand edge of the upper sheet and fold it down to the horizontal edge, making a firm crease only about half way along its length. Do the same on the other side, ensuring that this firm crease crosses the one on the other side.

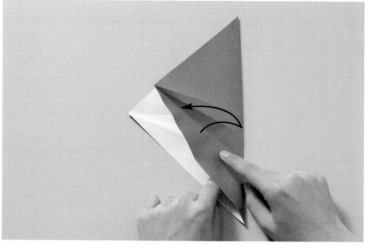

3 Now open out the sheet and make another crease between the two existing ones on both sides. Find the place by folding the existing angled crease up to the horizontal crease and pressing down—again only halfway across on both sides.

4 Open out the sheet and fold it in half from top to bottom to make a vertical crease.

5 Open out the sheet again then close it up by folding it along the middle of the three horizontal creases and pushing the two outer points round so that they meet at the back. The vertical crease will reverse, making an inside fold (see page 8).

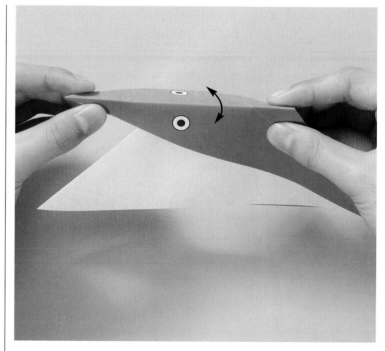

6 Fold the top of the head in half backward, making a new crease halfway between the eyes.

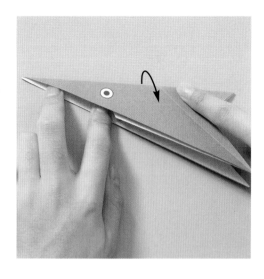

7 Turn the paper over, placing the two outer points on the table, then fold down the loose sheet behind the head making angled folded edges. Fold over the outer flaps so that the edges align along the edges of the object.

8 Fold the top of the object forward along the central crease.

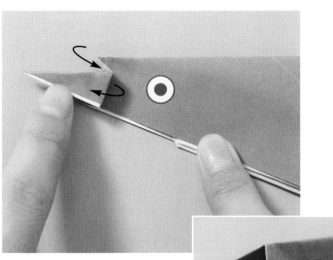

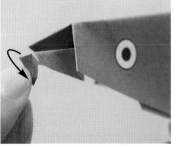

9 Fold over the nose twice to make a concertina fold and reverse the creases inside the object, then fold over the tip and turn it in on itself.

10 To finish, fold the two right-hand tips inside the model and then hook them over each other to hold in place.

25 KANI CRAB

Make this fun crab to play with both at the seaside and when you get home. If you want to make a group in different sizes, prepare various papers—perhaps also in different colors. Begin the model using the triangle fold technique. Take care with the claws, which are angled from the back, and do not forget to fold the lower side of the shell at the end.

You will need
1 sheet of 6in (15cm) square paper

SEA WORLD

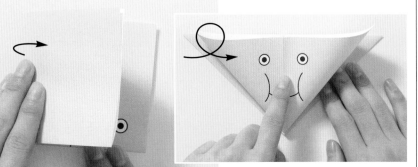

1 With the design face down, fold the sheet in half between the eyes and in half again, then lift the top flap and make a triangle fold (see page 9), repeating on the other side.

2 Fold the top flaps underneath themselves so that the outer tips now point down.

3 Turn the object over and fold down the top of the model, making a new crease about 1/8in (0.25cm) from the edge.

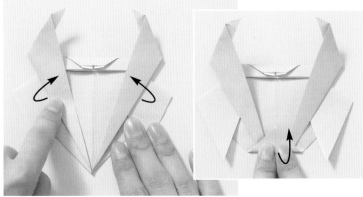

4 Fold the outer points up at an angle to make the crab's claws then turn up the bottom of the object to make a flat tail.

26 **EBI** LOBSTER

In Japan the lobster has long been revered as a bringer of luck. For instance, it is used as an offering at New Year and is a central part of a celebration party menu such as at a wedding. The long tendrils that are such a well-known characteristic of the lobster are called "whiskers" in Japan. Here they are made by cutting the *origami* paper with scissors.

You will need
1 sheet of 6in (15cm) square paper
Scissors

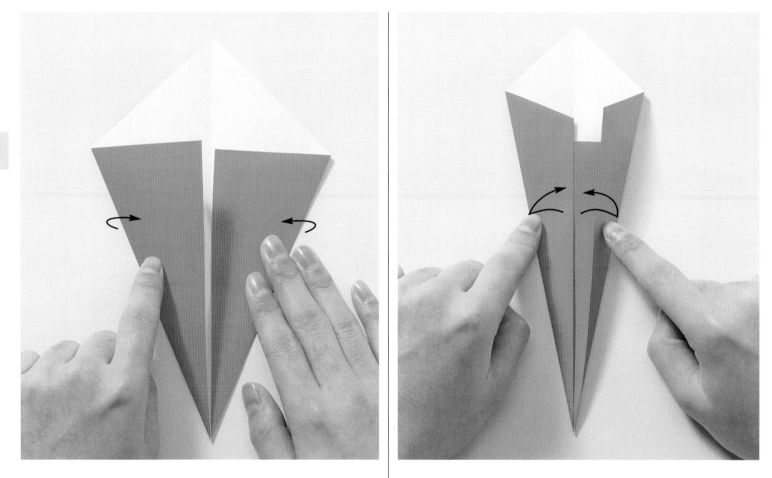

1 Fold the paper in half from corner to corner to make a crease, open out, then fold in the sides so that the lower side edges meet along the central crease.

2 Repeat by folding in the two side edges to make creases on both sides.

3 Fold the paper in half along the central crease.

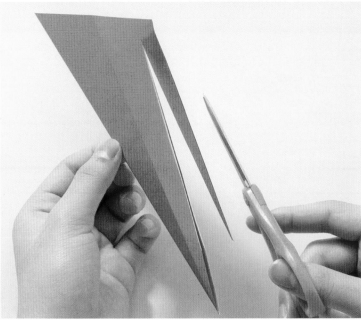

4 Use the scissors to make long cuts close to the outer edges of the paper, creating long thin spikes.

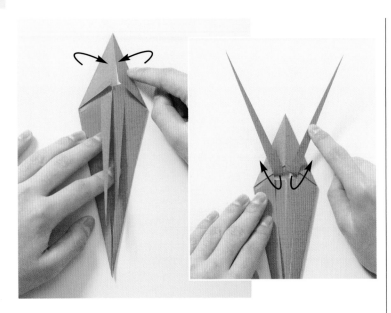

5 Open out the paper again and refold the creases made in step 2, then fold over the short diagonal edges at the top of the object so they meet down the center line and fold the two spikes forward.

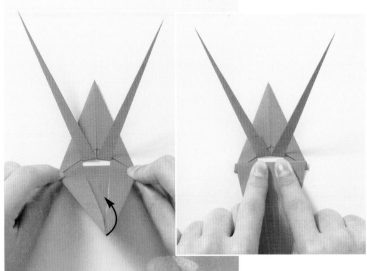

6 Fold forward the bottom half of the model, making a crease at its widest part, then fold the end back to make a ½in (1.25cm) wide concertina fold.

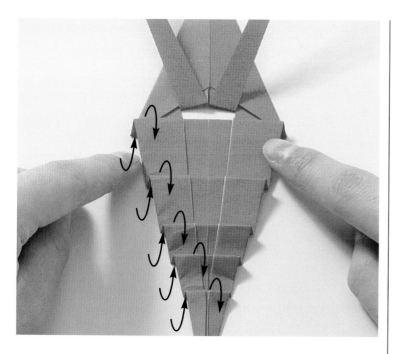

7 Make four more concertina folds at equal distances apart between the first fold and the tip of the tail.

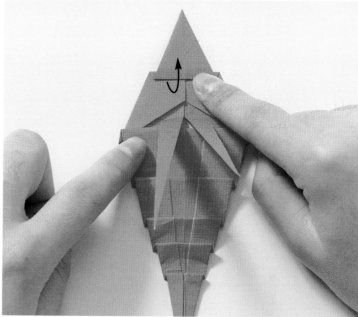

8 Temporarily fold back the spikes to give you room to make a concertina fold 1in (2.5cm) from the other end of the model.

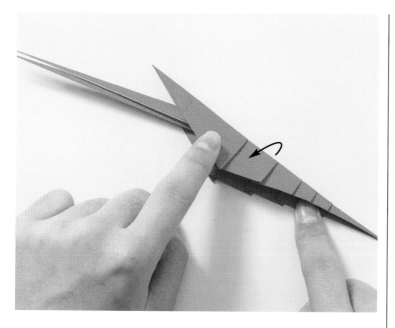

9 With the spikes again pointing outward, fold the model in half along the central crease.

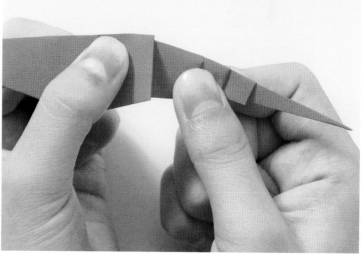

10 Gently manipulate the second largest concertina fold to make a curve between the model's body and tail.

27 SAME SHARK

Difficulty rating ● ● ●

You will need
1 sheet of 6in (15cm) square paper

The shark is an extraordinary part of the sea world, an animal that seems to have lived in the oceans for tens of thousands of years without evolving. These scary sharks with their open jaws and sharp teeth would strike fear into anything they encountered in the deep. They are made in a similar way to the most traditional *origami* model, the crane. The differences only start when those large jaws are created.

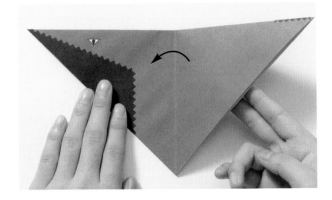

1 With the design face down, fold the sheet in half between the eyes and then in half again.

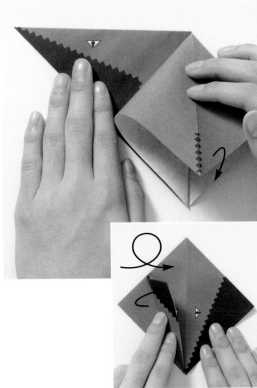

2 Lift the top flap and make a square fold (see page 9), repeating on the other side, then turn in the upper flaps so that the edges meet along the central crease.

3 Fold down the top triangle to make a horizontal crease then open up the folds and turn back the bottom tip, creating a long diamond shape.

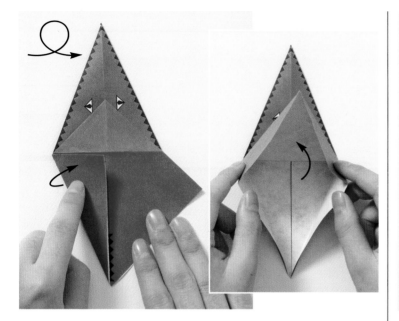
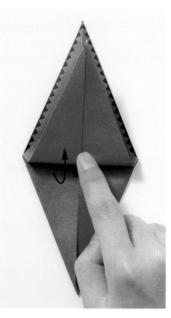

4 Turn the paper over and repeat—folding in the sides and making a crease across the top—before opening up the flaps and making another long diamond shape.

5 Turn back the top of the diamond then fold it forward again making a new crease about ½ in (1.25cm) below the existing crease.

6 Fold the upper flap on the right-hand side over toward the left.

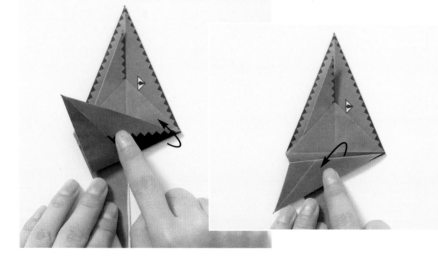
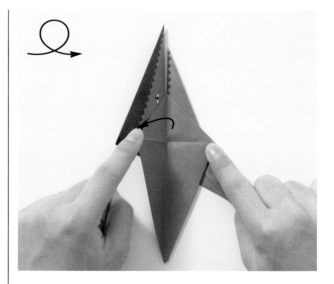

7 Lift up the upper flap at the bottom of the model and fold it forward at an angle, making a new crease across and down from the model's right-hand point. Next fold the same flap down making a crease along the line of the widest part of the object.

8 Turn the object over and fold the upper flap on the right-hand side over to the left.

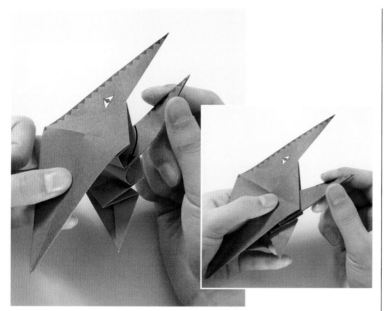

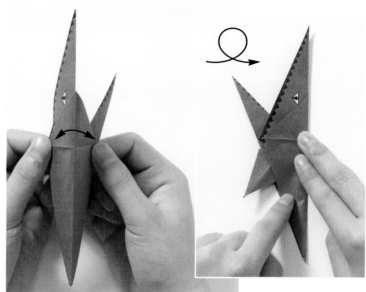

9 Lift up the object and carefully pull the lower jaw away from its original position, creating extra folds of paper inside the model, then press it flat again.

10 Lift the model and fold it in half along the central crease, turning it over so that the straight edge is now on its right-hand side.

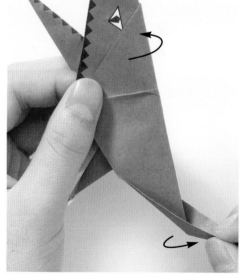

11 Open out the object again by turning the upper flap to the right, then form the shark's fin by pressing the sides together to halve its width and pressing it down flat.

12 Finish by turning up the bottom tip at an angle. Fold it inside the body and reverse the creases to create the tail.

FOREST

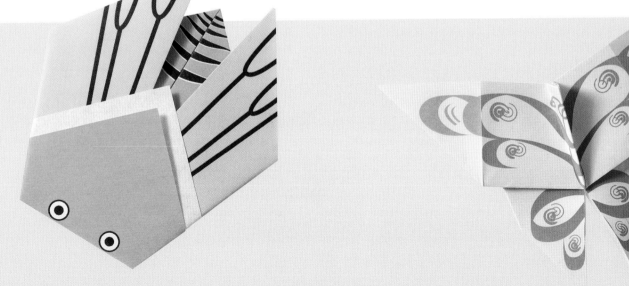

28 TENNTOUMUSHI LADYBIRD

The spectacular ladybird is one of the vivid insects in the forest, sometimes seen in large groups flying through the leaves and branches. Sadly, these *origami* ladybirds will never fly but you could use them as decoration near the window in your room, or put one on a greeting card to a friend. In addition, if you attach velour or felt and a pin to the reverse of the model, it can become a special *origami* brooch.

Difficulty rating ● ● ○

You will need
1 sheet of 6in (15cm) square paper

FOREST

1 Fold the paper from corner to corner across the design then turn the left and right points up to the top so that the bottom edges align up the middle of the paper. Fold down the upper tips, making creases across the middle of the model, to make a diamond shape.

2 Turn down both parts of the top tip, making a new crease just above the eyes. Fold both flaps inside the design, reversing the crease of the front flap.

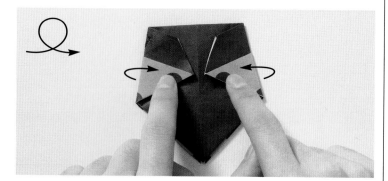

3 Turn the model over and fold in the two side points so that they meet at a slight angle in the center.

4 Open out the model and fold both flaps inside, reversing the creases. To finish turn over the sides of the head at a slight angle.

29 FUKURO OWL

Difficulty rating ● ○ ○

The owl is one of the best known characters of the forest, flying through the trees at night. What are they thinking about as their eyes shine out of the dark? This *origami* owl is made in the same way as the paper cup, one of the oldest traditional *origami* designs in Japan. Let's make many owls from paper of various sizes because it is so easy to create.

You will need
1 sheet of 6in (15cm) square paper

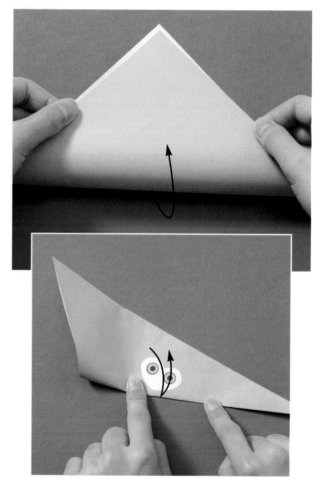

1 With the design face down and the eyes at the top, fold the bottom point up to the top, then fold the bottom edge up to sit on the right-hand edge, make a crease and open out.

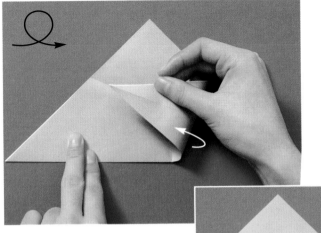

2 Fold the right-hand point over to the end of the crease made in the previous step, then fold the left-hand corner over to exactly the same point on the right-hand side.

3 Fold down the upper flap making a horizontal crease between the two side points, then turn the object over and fold forward the remaining flap before turning over the tip just below the eyes.

4 Turn the model over again and fold in the bottom corners at a slight angle to meet in the middle, then open out the bottom corners again, reverse the creases and fold inside.

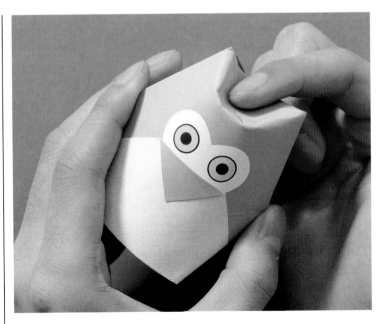

5 Gently push down the top of the model while squeezing the sides to open up the model and give it form.

30 BUTA GRASSHOPPER

Difficulty rating ● ● ●

You will need
1 sheet of 6in (15cm) square paper
Scissors

Let's go to the forest to make a real *origami* grasshopper. The powerful hind legs, which it uses to make incredible long-distance jumps, are clearly visible as are the wings and antennae. Cut these with scissors but take care not to make them too long. The method closely resembles that for the most well-known *origami* design, the crane, but once you start to fold the legs and wings the differences are clearly visible.

1 With the design face down and the eyes on the right, fold the top of the sheet down from corner to corner, then fold the right-hand point over to the left.

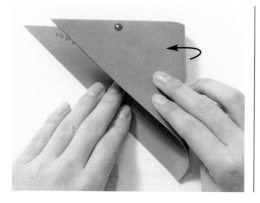

2 Lift the top flap and fold it down in a square fold (see page 9) then turn the model over and repeat on the other side so that you are left with a diamond shape.

3 Fold in the upper flaps on the back side of the model, then fold forward the top triangle to make a horizontal crease.

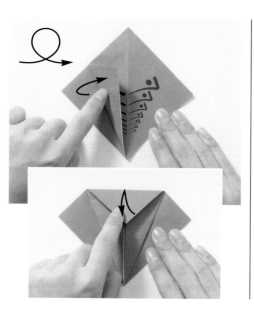

4 Next, open out the flaps and push the bottom point away from you, refolding the flap into a long diamond shape.

5 Lift the bottom left-hand flap and fold it away from you, making a crease between the center of the model and the outer point. Repeat on the right-hand side then fold the new flaps in half along a line from the bottom of the model to the top outer point, so that the lower edges meet in the middle.

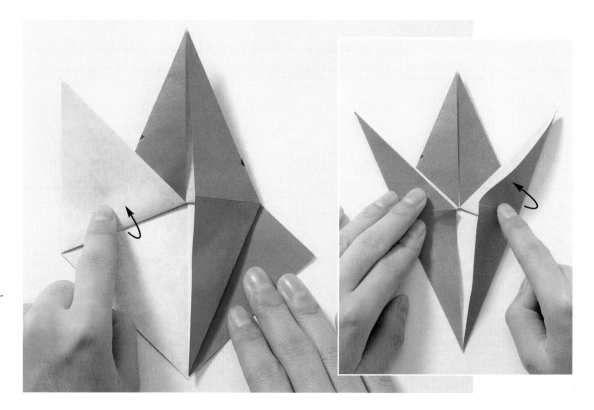

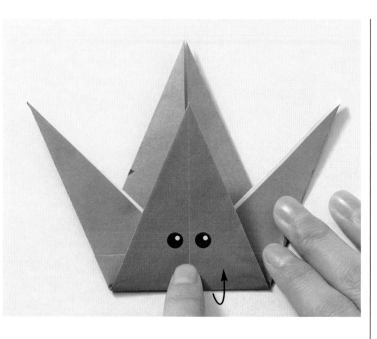

6 Turn up the bottom of the object, making the crease just below the center of the object.

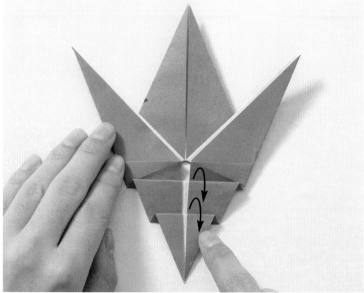

7 Make a concertina fold 1/8in (0.25cm) from the fold made in the previous step and repeat half way to the tip.

8 Use the scissors to make a ¼in (0.5cm) cut into the nearest crease to the tip on both sides, and also cut down the center of the tip to the first crease.

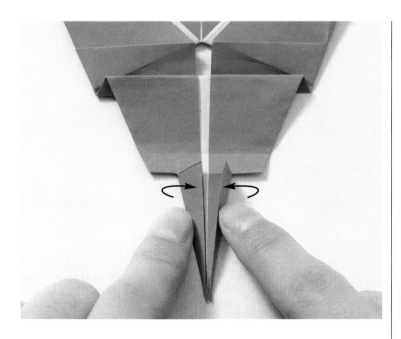

9 Fold in the two sides of the tip as far as the horizontal cuts will allow.

10 Fold the model in half along the central crease then fold back the spikes across the edge of the model to make the wings.

31 MOGURA MOLE

Difficulty rating ● ● ●

You will need
1 sheet of 6in (15cm) square paper

Go underground with this *origami* mole, digging through tunnels and burrowing its way deep into the soil. Although it can hardly see at all it never has a problem finding its way through the darkness. It's simple to make if you follow the step-by-step instructions but, unlike almost any other model, remember to start folding with the colored side of the *origami* paper facing upward. A happy mole will be completed after only a very simple series of folds.

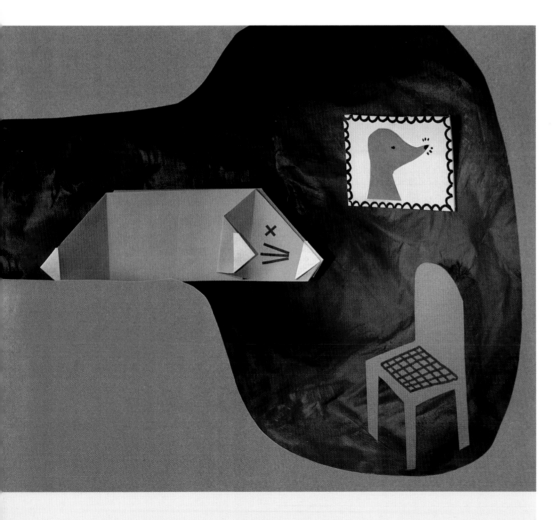

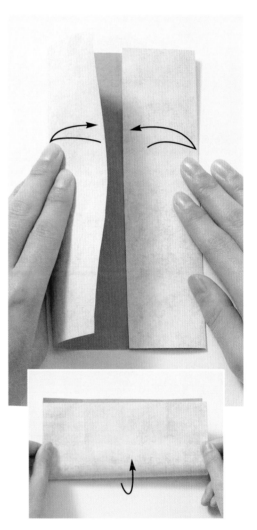

1 With the design face up, fold the paper in half and open out, then fold in both sides to meet in the middle and open out again. Fold the bottom up to the top.

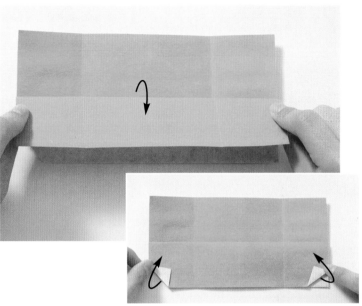

2 Fold over the bottom left-hand corner and make a crease, then open out the paper, fold the corner inside—reversing the creases—and close the paper.

3 Fold down the upper flap so the top runs along the bottom, then turn up the corners of the top sheet at the same angle as in the previous step.

4 Lift up the bottom left-hand corner and turn it across the object, refolding the flap to make a triangle fold (see page 9). Repeat on the right-hand side then turn the object over and repeat both folds.

5 Fold over the left-hand end of the model and make a vertical crease, then open up the back of the model and fold the end inside, reversing the creases.

32 **KOMADORI** ROBIN

Difficulty rating ● ● ○

The robin, with one of the loveliest, warbling songs in the forest, is especially associated with winter by the people in Europe—seeing it running with its red breast through the snow is a magical sight. The base of this *origami* model is the traditional Japanese small bird. As you start take care not to make a mistake with the location of the eyes. Afterwards, if each step is followed, a lovely robin will come to life.

You will need
1 sheet of 6in (15cm) square paper

FOREST

116

1 With the paper face down and the eyes at the top, fold the paper in half, then fold the sides in so that the lower edges meet along the central crease. Fold forward the top of the paper and tuck it inside the flaps.

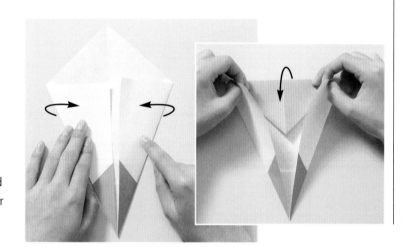

2 Fold down the side points so that the top edges also meet exactly along the central crease.

3 Lift and open the flaps, reversing the diagonal crease and refolding, so that the corner now points down and out from the object.

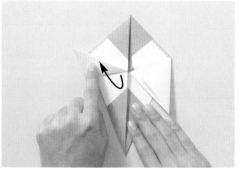

4 Turn up the points made in the last step, aligning the bottom edges along the diagonal crease line to the outer corners.

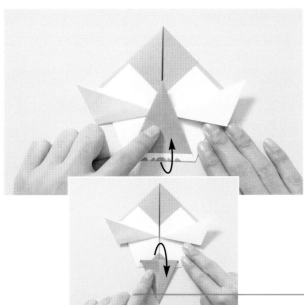

5 Fold up the bottom point so that the tip just crosses the edge of the design, then make a concertina fold approximately ½ in (1.25cm) nearer the tip.

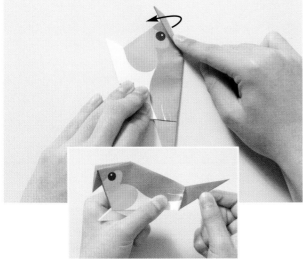

6 Fold the model in half along the central crease, then turn over the top of the head and make an inside fold. Gently prise up the tail to make an angle away from the body.

33 KATATASUMURI SNAIL

The snail is a relative of the sea animals that has come to live on land. They like the rainy season—perhaps because of a yearning to return to the sea where their ancestors lived. They also seem to enjoy relaxing among the grass and leaves as they slowly move through the forest. As this is a traditional design that has existed for a long time in Japan it's a good chance to master an ancient *origami* model.

Difficulty rating ● ● ●

You will need
1 sheet of 6in (15cm) square paper

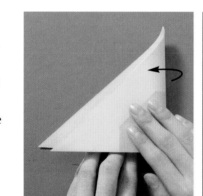

1 With the design face down, fold the top of the sheet up from corner to corner then fold the right-hand point over to the left.

2 Lift the top flap and fold it down in a square fold (see page 9) then turn the model over and repeat this on the other side so that you are left with a diamond shape.

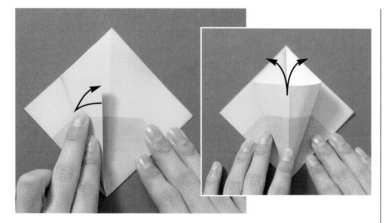

3 Fold in the upper flap on the left-hand side so that the edge runs down the center line and make a crease, then lift up the flap, open it out and refold it symmetrically across the object.

4 Turn over the right-hand part of the flap made in the previous step and fold in the upper flap on the right-hand side of the object, before also opening it out and refolding as before.

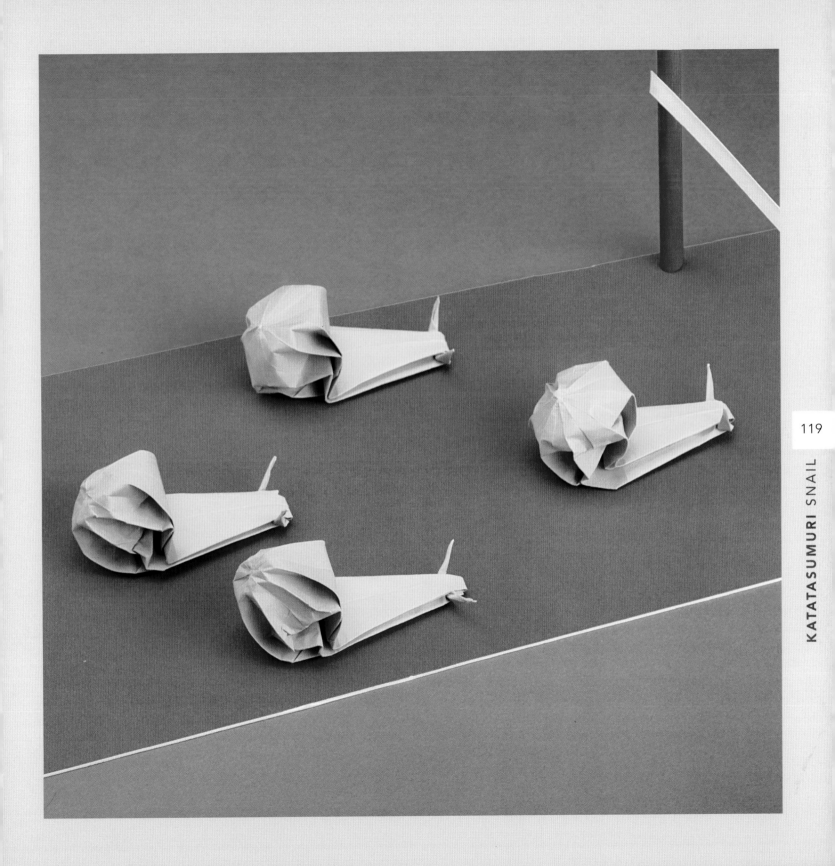

5 Turn the flap over to the left as before and fold in the final flap on the left-hand side, before also opening it out and refolding.

6 Now turn all the folded flaps back to the right so that only one, unfolded flap is on the left. Fold this into the center and open out as before.

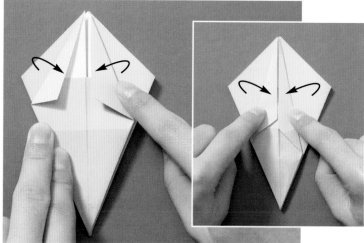

7 Lift up the object by the folded flaps and press together the two remaining flaps. Now turn the object and fold over two flaps to make both sides even, then replace on the table ensuring that a white triangle is visible.

8 Fold over the upper flap on the right-hand side so that the edge runs down the central crease, and fold over the upper flap on the left-hand side so that the edge runs down half way towards the central crease. Turn over both edges so that they meet along the central crease.

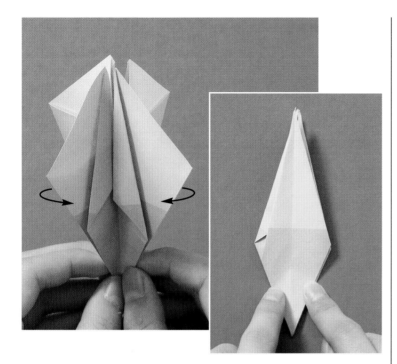

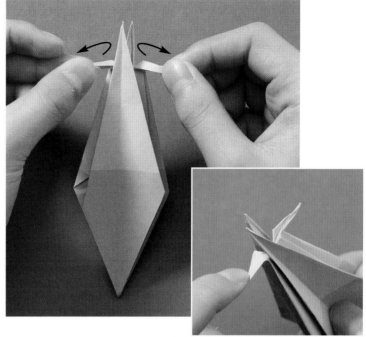

9 Turn the object over and repeat, then lift the object and turn it in your hands until two white triangles are again showing. Repeat the folding process from the previous step. You should be left with a narrow diamond-shaped object with solid paper at the front and back.

10 Take the loose points inside at the top and fold them both outward at right angles. Reverse these folds and tuck the ends inside.

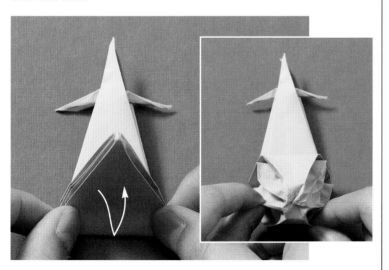

11 Fold up the wide end of the object and gently prise the paper open to make the snail's shell.

12 Bend the narrow end over and downward to make the snail's head.

34 **SEMI** CICADA

The cicada is an insect that has become famous as the traditional poetic symbol of the hot Japanese summer. Everybody can recall a day spent in the forest on holiday when they hear the cicada's cry during the heat. This model resembles the traditional *origami* design for the helmet that was worn by the *samurai*. Because it is so very easy to make, even a small child will be able to master the challenge.

Difficulty rating ● ● ○

You will need
1 sheet of 6in (15cm) square paper

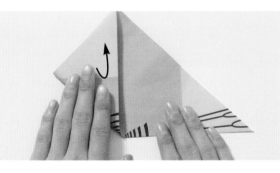

1 With the design face down and the eyes at the top, fold the top of the sheet up from corner to corner, then fold both side points up to the top point so that the bottom edges align up the middle of the object.

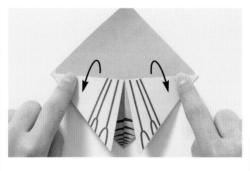

2 Turn down these flaps, making slightly angled fold lines from the outer points, ensuring the tips break out from the bottom edges of the object.

3 Turn down the upper flap at the top making a fold line about ½in (1.25cm) above the outer points, then fold over the remaining top flap making the crease a further ⅛in (0.25cm) above the center line.

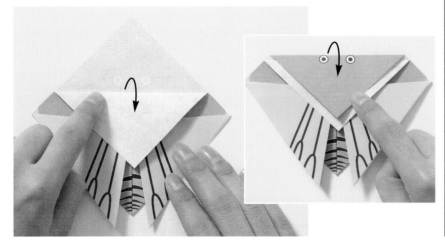

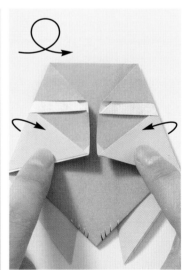

4 Turn the model over and fold in the side points at an angle so that the short edges meet along the center of the model.

35 **CHO** BUTTERFLY

The butterfly might be the most beautiful, mysterious insect in the world. The forest is a haven for many brightly colored varieties, each of a different size and with a different design on its wings. It has naturally been loved for its beauty and has become a wonder to be collected and treasured. The way to make this butterfly is the same as the traditional *origami* model ship, though with a strong crease to indicate its head.

Difficulty rating ● ● ○

You will need
1 sheet of 6in (15cm) square paper

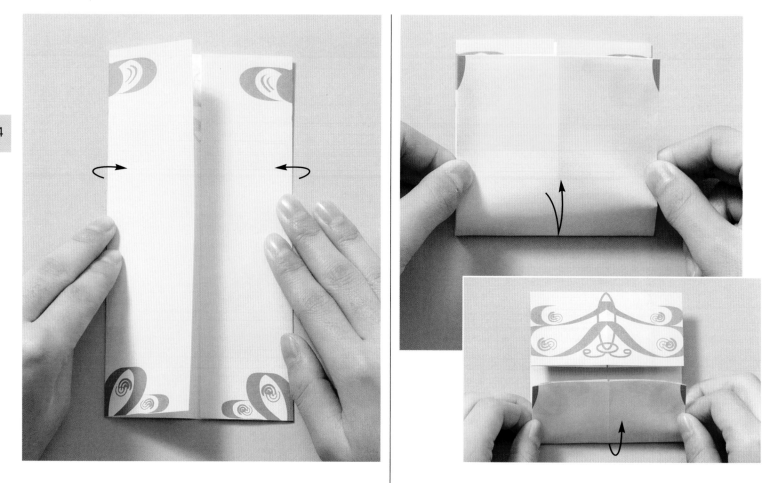

1 With the design face down, fold the sheet in half to make a crease, then open out and fold both edges in to meet in the center.

2 Fold the bottom to the top to make a crease, then open out and fold the top and bottom edges to meet in the center.

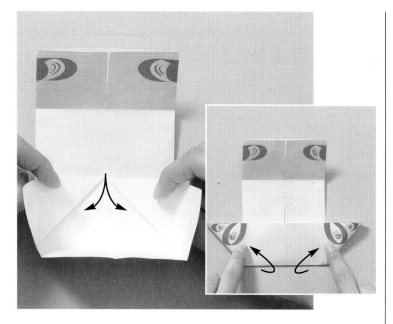

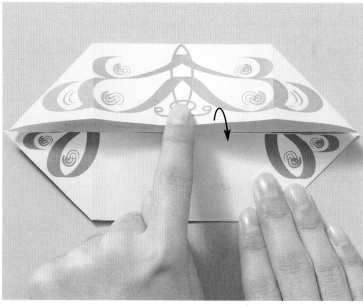

3 Open out the bottom flap and push the corners of the paper out, refolding the sheet flat to make a triangle on both sides of the object.

4 Repeat on the top flap. Ensure that you can see the entirety of the design.

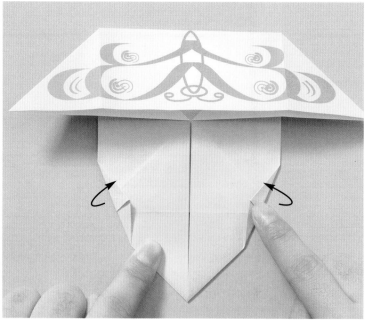

5 Turn the lower flaps forward, making fold lines between the middle of the model and the bottom corners.

6 Fold in the side points of the bottom flaps at a slight angle, ensuring that both sides are identical.

7 Turn the object over and fold over the wide part of the model along the central crease.

8 Turn the object back over and fold in half lengthwise.

9 Keeping a finger on the bottom left-hand corner, fold the top flap forward at an angle and make a crease.

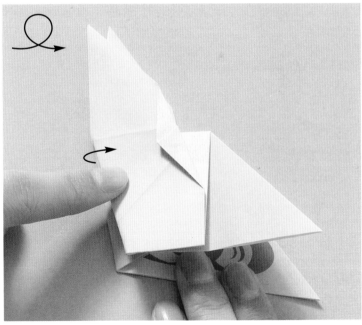

10 To finish, turn the object over and make a crease on the other side to match the one made in the previous step.

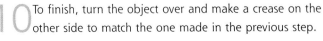

SUPPLIERS

Origami paper is available at most good paper stores or online. Try searching online for "origami paper" to find a whole rang of stores, selling a wide variety of paper, that will send packages directly to your home.

UK
HOBBYCRAFT
www.hobbycraft.co.uk
TEL: +44 (0)1202 596100

JP-BOOKS
www.jpbooks.co.uk
c/o Mitsukoshi, Dorland House
TEL: +44 (0)20 7839 4839
info@jpbooks.co.uk

JAPAN CENTRE
www.japancentre.com
TEL: 020 3405 1150
bookshop_manager@japancentre.com

THE JAPANESE SHOP (online only)
www.thejapaneseshop.co.uk
info@thejapaneseshop.co.uk

USA
A.C. MOORE
www.acmoore.com
Stores nationwide
TEL: 1-888-226-6673

CRAFTS, ETC.
www.craftsetc.com
Online store
TEL: 1-800-888-0321

HOBBY LOBBY
www.hobbylobby.com
Stores nationwide

JO-ANN FABRIC AND CRAFT STORE
www.joann.com
Stores nationwide
TEL: 1-888-739-4120

MICHAELS STORES
www.michaels.com
Stores nationwide
TEL: 1-800-642-4235

HAKUBUNDO (HONOLULU, HAWAII)
www.hakubundo.com
TEL: (808)947-5503
hakubundo@hakubundo.com

FRANCE
CULTURE JAPON S.A.S.
www.boutiqueculturejapon.fr
TEL: +33 (0)1 45 79 02 00
culturejpt@wanadoo.fr

BOOKS
The Simple Art of Japanese Papercrafts by Mari Ono (CICO Books)
Origami for Children by Mari Ono and Roshin Ono (CICO Books)
Fly, Origami, Fly by Mari Ono and Roshin Ono (CICO Books)
Kantan Origami 100 part 2 by Kazuo Kobayashi (Nihon Vogue-Sha Co.Ltd.)
Ugokasu Tobasu Origami by Seibido Shuppan Editorial Department (Seibido Shuppan Co., Ltd.)

WEBSITES
Origami Club: en.origami-club.com
Papillon Origami (Japanese only): www.mb.ccnw.ne.jp/sakurako/papillon
Origami Kaikan: origamikaikan.co.jp/info/e_index.html
Japan Origami Academic Society: www.origami.gr.jp/index-e.html
Nippon Origami Association: www.origami-noa.com/index_e.htm
ORIGAMI USA: www.origami-usa.org
British Origami Society: www.britishorigami.info

ORIGAMI DESIGN CREDITS

Special thanks to the origami masters who consented to the inclusion of their original ideas in this book:
Baby bear, Eagle, Zebra, Elephant, Giraffe, Monkey, Lion, Chameleon, Snake, Leopard, Sea otter, Whale, Sea turtle, Penguin, Crab, Mole by Fumiaki Shingu at www.origami-club.com
Gorilla, Shark by Taiko Niwa
Lobster by Kazuo Kobayashi
Panda by Minako Ishibashi

INDEX

ACKNOWLEDGMENTS

When making a book there are so many people to thank. At the top of the list is Cindy Richards, whose idea this book was. Thanks to her unremitting interest and encouragement, this opportunity became a wonderfully enriching experience. Thanks also to my editor, Robin Gurdon, whose helpfulness and competent direction meant a lot to me. Thanks to Geoff Dann for his friendliness and for displaying the greatest patience during photography. It was a wonderful experience as ever to spend a week working with him. Many thanks also to Sally Powell, Pete Jorgensen, and Paul Tilby, and to Trina Dalziel, who designed the backgrounds for all projects. This book became a very happy book through her wonderful sensibility, I wish to express my gratitude to her. Friends and family have been tremendously supportive, in particular Takumasa, my husband, who has designed wonderful origami papers for this book. And our son, Roshin, for acting as the model for all the projects, and also helping with my texts. I cannot thank them enough for their encouragement.